To Valarie –
Best Wishes!
– *(signature)*

REGULAR
& *Decaf*

REGULAR
& *Decaf*

One Friend with Schizophrenia
One Friend with Bipolar
One Ongoing Conversation
One Cup at a Time

ANDREW D. GADTKE

Risen Man Publishing, LLC
Edina, Minnesota

Regular & Decaf
One Friend with Schizophrenia, One Friend with Bipolar, One
Ongoing Conversation, One Cup at a Time
By Andrew D. Gadtke

Risen Man Publishing, LLC
P.O. Box 24893
Edina, MN 55424

ISBN: 978-0-9816183-0-2

For my mother...
because she loves me even
when I'm unlovable

Disclaimer—Note to the Reader

This book was not created by a mental health professional. No professional advice or prescription for action is intended in what follows. Please consult your mental health professional for such advice. Although psychiatric terminology is used in what follows, the accuracy of such terminology has not been guaranteed. The conversations are real and were recorded, transcribed, and then later turned into prose dialog. They have not been edited for content, only for clarity. The content of the conversations is based exclusively on the memories of the participants.

TABLE OF CONTENTS

Chapter 1:
Introduction

People don't know the real story. They only know what they have observed from the outside. Their version goes like this: Andrew was an intelligent, hardworking young man. In 1999 he graduated high school tied for first in his class, and then he went away to study at a prestigious university. He came home from college one summer, and he was different. Since then, he hasn't been in school and hasn't been working, and instead just sits around all day long. He says it has something to do with an unseen illness.

The real version goes like this: I was an intelligent, hardworking young man. I went away to study at college. While there, I started having terrifying visual and auditory hallucinations. I became fearful of government agents who were trying to kill me. I grew increasingly apathetic and paranoid. I later learned that this was just the start of the development of the most debilitating mental illness known to man.

Nowadays, most people think I'm just crazy. They don't see

me as a real person who had aspirations and dreams of my own. I am the butt of jokes and the cause of fears. I am a young man with SPMI—severe and persistent mental illness. Although SPMI is never talked about at social dinner parties, there are millions of us out there. We are the young adults who have dropped out of college to live in the basements of our parents' houses. We are the middle-aged bachelors living in filthy one-room apartments in low-rent neighborhoods. We are the old homeless who have been surviving on the streets for decades. We stink. We are weird. We offend polite people's sensibilities.

I've met many other people with SPMI who are far more ill than me. If their cognitive impairment is minimal and we can carry on a conversation, I freely offer my empathy. Whenever I meet the sickest of the sick, however, there's a question lurking in the back of my mind: Do they still have a soul? Is it intact or has it been destroyed by mental illness? It might be a weird question, but I wonder what happens when everything that makes a person human is destroyed. Has the ghost died inside the machine, or is it still there, simply imprisoned inside by the illness? I feel my soul is still alive, and so I reason that theirs must be too. But that only begs another question: If they do have a soul, then why do others treat them as if they didn't?

The answer, it seems to me, is that no one understands the tragic change that occurs when someone develops SPMI. Severe and persistent mental illness indiscriminately strikes normal people with hopes and dreams—and then turns their lives into a living hell. What precisely that hell will be like no one really knows; the outcome is different for each person. There are many available statistics, however, and plenty of evidence as to what the average course will be like for any particular mental illness. It may just be my paranoia, but it seems to me that the psychiatrists know this average prognosis well, but they keep it hidden from the people with mental illness and from their families.

When I first went into treatment for my mental health problem, I was told by my psychiatrist at the time that they don't give diagnoses, they just treat symptoms. It was a partial lie. They do regularly label people with diagnoses; it was simply her practice not to tell her patients what they were. Not telling patients their diagnoses is an old practice that is on its way out, but from my experience it seems to have been replaced by another equally appalling practice—hiding the prognosis instead of the diagnosis. In my thinking, this is because the psychiatrists who know the average outcome feel that if you knew your prognosis you would kill yourself. It seems almost all SPMI information is kept hidden from patients and families and the population at large. I often wonder if the mentally ill would be treated more humanely if regular people knew the doom-and-gloom prognosis, the tragic outcome of SPMI. If normal people knew that fate could take a regular person and force him or her to live a life of horror, would they be more empathetic?

I have found a few general statistics about my mental illness, and from my level of functioning I had approximated what my prognosis was soon after being diagnosed. Apparently the psychiatrists were right after all, because it did make me want to kill myself.

Not long after being diagnosed, I reasoned the following to be my prognosis:

Every single dream of mine will go unrealized, and I will never be able to do anything meaningful with my life. I will never be able to do the schoolwork necessary to finish college. I will never have any career, and in fact I will never even be able to hold down a menial job.

I will have no friends, and it will be impossible to make new ones. People won't like to share my company anymore. I won't converse with anyone but my family and doctors for the rest of my life. I will become so lonely that I will doubt that there is a God. I won't even be able to trust my own family members. I will never have a family of my own—never getting married and never having children. I will never even be able to get a date. I will be celibate for the rest of my life.

I will never have any interests again, and I won't enjoy any activity. I won't have the concentration to read a book or watch television. My days will be filled with rocking and pacing, and I will be unbearably bored.

My teeth will yellow and rot from smoking excessively. The medicines will make me obese, and I will probably develop diabetes. The meds might also make me grow breast tissue and make me impotent. I will have an increased risk of heart disease. I will become addicted to caffeine and nicotine and possibly illegal drugs. I will never exercise and will become completely sedentary. My life expectancy will shorten by about 25 years from my poor physical health.

I will be fearful all the time for the rest of my life. I will hear voices that ridicule me. I will see visions that terrify me. I will not be able to make eye contact with people, and I will become very weird. I will become hyperreligious and might cut off my hand or pluck out my eye because I think that is what Jesus wants me to do to avoid sin. I will never have any joy ever again. I will hardly ever shower, and I will never brush my teeth. I will start to stink. My personality will change, and I will want to spend all my time alone. I will have a hard time conversing with people. I will obsessively write meaningless thoughts. I might not be able to concentrate enough to speak coherently.

I might become homeless and have to eat from a dumpster. I will never be able to trust my own thoughts, and I will never know what is real with any certainty. People will probably treat me poorly, and I will pray every night for death. I will get progressively worse. And finally, I will die by suicide within five years.

I've been aware of this doom-and-gloom prognosis since I was diagnosed three and a half years ago, but I have been struggling against it since my first symptoms appeared almost eight years ago. Severe and persistent mental illness is just that—severe and persistent. It negatively affects every aspect of your life, and it never goes away. I do believe, however, that there is cause for hope. Despite all the hardship, you can have a life worth living. It will be difficult and might require you to reevaluate your value system, but it is possible. New treatments are on the horizon, so maybe the prognosis will improve soon. All I can say is take it a day at a time. Just relax and have a coffee.

CHAPTER 2:
SCHIZOPHRENIA
AND BIPOLAR DISORDER

I used to like Caribou Coffee better; however, since I can now get to Starbucks by taking roads that are easier for me to drive, I find the vanilla lattes at Starbucks more to my liking. I'm not really into driving anymore, because everything comes at you too fast. Luckily, the route to Starbucks is easy. I went there this morning and had, of course, a vanilla latte. A barista asked me what I did for a living, and I said I'm a writer. However, I'm not really a writer. I'm not really anything. I once read on the Internet that it is a good idea for people like me to say things like that. I say I'm a writer, but I could just as easily say that I work freelance as a computer programmer. With my background in science, math, and technology, that response would probably be the smarter thing to say. It certainly is more believable to others. I have made two charcoal drawings in my life, so I suppose I could tell people I'm an artist. Regardless, I like writer best. I never know if people are buying the story I'm telling them, but I don't think it matters. Anything is better than telling them the truth.

It isn't that I'm embarrassed about the truth, because I eventually tell most people I know—all except the women I'm interested in dating. I hesitate to tell people the truth because the truth makes some people feel uncomfortable—or worse, makes them feel afraid of me. Even when the right time comes to tell someone, the moment is still awkward. Nevertheless, instead of having a rehearsed script of how I tell people, I play it by ear. Sometimes I say I have a brain disease, while other times I say I'm a mad genius. To help them better understand my condition, I will often ask them if they have seen the movie *A Beautiful Mind*, which is about the mathematics genius John Nash and his life with mental illness. No matter how the conversation starts, it always ends with me revealing my diagnosis—paranoid schizophrenia.

I have found that a lot of people think severe mental illness is similar to mental retardation and that you have it from birth. I have also found that many of the normal people assisting those with a mental illness don't understand it at all. Even family members who have cared for their mentally ill relatives for many years rarely understand the first thing about mental illness. Truth be told, sometimes even I don't understand my own illness.

Although I have access to everything that I am experiencing, I must try to understand my illness using a broken brain. That's what makes mental illness so complex. Only people who have experienced a severe mental illness are in a position to report about it; however, they are usually too ill to share what is occurring inside their heads.

I wasn't always mentally ill. As a kid, I was a little different, but almost always in a positive way. In most regards I was a typical kid. Like most kids, I had friends throughout my childhood, and in high school I dated several girls. Although I was slightly better than average in athletics, my potential came into full bloom in academics. I chose the most advanced courses available and got As in every class. I was on the quiz bowl team, was a co-captain of the math team, and was a member of the National Honor Society. When I graduated from high school I was tied for first in my class of 600 students.

However, that stage of my life is all past now. No longer am I the high-adrenaline, high-achieving, type-A person I once was. I do not think that I'm worse. Instead, I'm different, and in my opinion, probably better. Most people probably wouldn't agree with that, and they might think that my describing myself as different was a bit of an understatement. I prefer to think of myself as quirky. That is just semantics, I suppose. But in reality, I am who I am now, and most people have been very kind to me. Today, people like me are treated much better than in the past. You had to conceal your illness back then. Otherwise, you would be treated rather harshly. I still can't get a date, but the people who know I'm ill have been very nice to me.

Despite their pleasantries, no one with a normal brain can understand me. I take responsibility for their lack of understanding; I simply have been unable to relate to normal people what I have to go through on a daily basis. Since it is a communication problem, I doubt that anyone but a poet could convey in words a true understanding of the depth of mental illness. Not being a poet myself, it might seem foolhardy for me even to attempt to communicate my experiences to someone who hasn't experienced mental illness. How can the rational understand the irrational; the ordered, the disordered; and the sane, the insane? You can call me foolhardy then, and I will take the criticism seriously. During the past year, however, I have been giving speeches to community groups around the Twin Cities, and although I won't say that I have been able to convey a deep understanding of mental illness to my audiences, I have created sparks of understanding.

You see, I have a need to be understood. In the past I thought it futile to even try to get someone to understand the horrors I have lived through, and so I have tried to suppress my need to be understood. But as a real need, it has festered under the surface. I know others who feel the same. Whenever I get together with other mentally ill people, the first topic to be broached is our illnesses and symptoms, and I find great relief in knowing that someone else can relate or in the very least, empathize with me.

The first day I met my friend Benji, we were going to a National Alliance on Mental Illness (NAMI) support group to find others who could relate to our experiences. After the support group, Benji and I went for coffee at 50th and France in Edina, Minn., to chat about our lives in more detail. This chat led to a friendship and a dialog about our illnesses that continues to this day.

Right now I am back at Starbucks at 50th and France, and it is bustling as usual. Because it's mid-afternoon though, I was able to score a set of two plush chairs for Benji and me. I plop down into a seat, coffee in hand, and wait for him to join me. He is busy chatting with a female barista who is making his coffee. Coming to Starbucks for coffee is a near daily ritual for Benji and me, and I enjoy conversing with him because he has a life as peculiar as mine. He is my best friend, but I'm sure that he would quite readily point out that he is my only friend. Truth be told, I don't care to be around people much, and so I find one friend to be enough.

The 50th and France section of Edina is an upper-class area of an upper-class suburb of Minneapolis. The neighborhood is full of women's clothing stores, expensive spas and salons, and fine-dining restaurants. The movie theater runs only independent and foreign films. The sidewalks are populated mostly by retirees and aging trophy wives with their teenage daughters. Benji and I feel at home here, however, because, through no fault of our own, we were born into Minnesota's upper class.

Benji finally approaches and grabs a seat. He is 6 foot 2 with a regular build and fair skin. I think he is German by ancestry, but he looks like he also has some Scandinavian blood. I'm German by ancestry too, but I'm short and stocky, standing only 5 feet 8 inches tall. I ask him if he is ready, and he nods yes. So I turn on my tape recorder and set it on the coffee table.

"It is Friday," I say toward the microphone, "and Benji and I are sitting in Starbucks. This is the first of our recorded conversations about life, about our lives."

"*Very difficult lives,*" Benji interjects.

I nod my head in enthusiastic agreement. "Very difficult lives—exactly."

Starbucks has taken on a particular significance in my life, and I think in Benji's life too. It's our meeting place, for sure, but for me this place is special because, while here, I can relax and forget about the troubles of my life. In the past, and I suppose in some instances even now, the local pub would have played that role. But for me, the local coffee shop is the best. When I'm here, I'm normal. I'm just like everyone else. Quite often, but only when I'm by myself, I completely forget about diagnoses and medications. I'm just me, and I'm normal. Rarely does the normal me—or the former me, if that is more correct—shine through. My mother can tell in my smile and in my eyes if I am in a normal state. My true self shines through when I'm thinking of philosophical theories, when I'm listening to good music, and when I'm drinking a great coffee.

I take a sip of my usual coffee, a tall, nonfat vanilla latte. Since I'm already 35 lbs. overweight, I always go with the nonfat milk because the medicines cause weight gain. "Benji, what are you drinking?"

He sets his drink down. *"Decaf, of course, because I don't drink caffeine—caramel macchiato."*

"Why don't you drink caffeine?"

In a playful way, he says, *"Because it makes me go crazy."* He takes a breath and becomes a little more serious. *"It's bad for my bipolar disorder."*

"That's formerly known as manic-depressive illness?" I ask.

"Yes. It's a mood disorder."

"I consume tons of caffeine," I say, "lots of coffee. It's because I have schizophrenia, and caffeine is a huge addiction for people like me. I just crave coffee. I've heard some people with my illness drink like 40 cups of coffee a day. I'm nowhere near that excessive."

I wouldn't say that I'm addicted to caffeine, but I use it to fight the sedation caused by my antipsychotic medications.

"Yeah, well . . . you're regular and I'm decaf."
I chuckle. "My mother told me the other day that when she describes you to people, she says that you are the opposite of me: You are good with people, you like people, you are charismatic, and you like doing things. That's unlike me, who just sort of sits around all day. That's how she describes you. It's pretty funny."
"How would you describe yourself?" Benji asks.
"I don't do too much. I am 26 and single. I don't have a job. I used to go to school—I went to a lot of different schools. I started out at the California Institute of Technology—Caltech, and next to the University of Wisconsin, then to Iowa State University, and finally to the University of Minnesota. I was thinking about going back to school, but just recently decided not to. My interests are mostly in philosophy and theology, really impractical. You can't do anything with them. But they are fun, because I spend most of my time thinking about things." I readjust my position in the chair. "How would you describe yourself?"
"Twenty-four years old," Benji says, *"not accomplished."*
"But you want to be?" I ask him.
Benji lowers his voice. *"Maybe I've given up, I don't know. I had big dreams and they failed, and then I had big dreams again and they failed. Now my dreams are small, so hopefully I won't fail."*

"You're in school right now?"

"I managed to make it through college," Benji says.

"Where did you go?

"Miami University in Oxford, Ohio."

"What did you study," I ask him.

"Botany, economics, interdisciplinary studies, and business management."

I'm thinking it is quite a list. "What did you get your degree in?"

"Management. That was the easiest. That was my scapegoat so I could just graduate. But I'm back in school again, because after a whole summer of unemployment and interviewing, I gave up on finding a job in the field of business. Now I want to be a landscape designer."

A smile comes across Benji's face. *"And I picked that because— it is laid back,"* he says with emphasis as he puts his arms behind his head. *"I need that. I can't handle dealing with stressful environments anymore because of my illness."*

"What happens when you are under stress?" I ask. "Increasing symptoms?"

"Yeah, I start getting delusional and not sleeping, or I get completely unmotivated and depressed."

I've seen Benji get symptomatic, and I'm happy that today he looks like he is healthy, the best I've ever seen him. "We have been having these conversations for about how long? Two years?"

"Two years."

"Do you remember how we met?" I ask.

"The only reason we met was because a friend of my mom knew

a friend of your mom, who said, 'My kid is home from school because he had to take a medical withdrawal, and he has no friends at home.' My mom's friend of the friend said, 'I know someone who has a kid at home who is sick and who has no friends either, so maybe these guys would make good friends.'"

"So we got set up on a play date to go to a NAMI support group."

"Pretty much." Benji laughs. *"Well, we were both aspiring writers at the time."*

"That's right. We were going to write a screenplay together."

"Still want to."

"Maybe that is still in the cards."

Every so often, whenever neither of us is doing well, we start writing a screenplay. So far it has never worked out. The screenplay is always about mental illness, and usually it is a mix of reality and fiction. I always suggest that Benji be cast as the main character. For a screenplay to work, the audience needs to like the main character, and Benji is very likeable. I think I was likeable before I got ill, but I don't feel that I am anymore.

When I was in high school I was never a social butterfly, but I was quite social. I had a few close friends and many more acquaintances. I considered myself to be the leader of the nerds, but because I played football I could float between the high school cliques and get along in any group. People generally liked my company. I always had a smile on my face, and my good nature rubbed off on people. I was interested in knowing everything there was to learn, and I would be very engaging to others in conversations. I could talk intelligently on any topic from current events and politics to science and the arts.

With this illness, however, all that changed. I lost interest in almost everything. I didn't follow current events or politics, and I had no intelligent thoughts on science or the arts. Much of the time I had no thoughts whatsoever. In conversations with people I generally had nothing to add, and so I didn't talk much. While I was engaging before, now people preferred that I kept my mouth shut. When I did open my mouth, I often stammered and said weird things that were a product of an ill mind. My sense of humor was dying off, as was my passion for anything and everything.

My loss of interests had made me a very boring person, and as such I was bored almost continuously. My personality had completely changed, and I had become an extreme introvert. I didn't even know how to interact with people anymore, and I didn't care to.

I remember talking to a couple with a new born baby a few months ago. They were doing most of the chatting, and I was content listening to them tell me about how fast their baby boy was growing. But it became apparent in the conversation that I would have to say something lighthearted, and so with a deadpan expression, I asked if the baby could discuss philosophy yet. No one found my joke funny, and it created a silence awkward enough to end the conversation. Many people tell bad jokes, but it is being just a little bit off socially that stands out and makes communication with people awkward.

I decide to move the subject away from the screenplay: "Tell me how a doctor, a psychiatrist, would describe bipolar," I ask. "What would he or she say that illness is?"

Mainly, a person normally has a range of emotions—from happiness to eternal sadness. However, a person with bipolar disorder basically has a wider spectrum of emotions from happy to sad. Beyond the wider range of emotions, a bipolar person can also experience extreme mood swings. These moods can jump from one to the other very rapidly; one moment you're feeling very happy and the next moment you're so unhappy that you can't get out of bed. It makes feeling normal mostly sad because you know how happy you can feel and how driven you can feel when you are in the epiphany of the emotions when you are manic.

"When you get really happy it is called the manic state?" I ask him.

"Yeah," Benji says, *"it used to be called manic depression. There is the manic state, which is like a natural high, below that is the hypomanic state, and then there is the normal state. Next, the low state is mild depression, and finally, the lowest state is severe depression."*

"What are some of the things someone might do or think in the manic state?"

"Might get delusional, might hallucinate."

"That's an extreme manic state," I say.

He continues. *"They might be irresponsible with finances."*

"Going on spending sprees?"

"They might," he says.

I can see that he is thinking of other behaviors, but nothing seems to be coming to his mind. "Does it sort of feel like being high on drugs?"

"*Yeah.*"

"But you're not on drugs."

Benji shakes his head, affirming he isn't on drugs. *"It's like a big cocaine binge,"* he says with a smile.

"What about the other extreme, the depression?" I ask. "What is that like?"

"It's like withdrawal from heroin," he says with a huge laugh. *"I've never done heroin, though. Basically, you can't get out of bed. You have lack of self esteem, lack of direction, lack of appetite. Sometimes you have an increased appetite, but that is usually from meds. Lack of appetite goes along with depression. You have an inability to put anything together, or even go outside, get out of bed, or eat a meal."*

"That's interesting," I say to him.

"Thank you, thank you, doctor," Benji says to me in a sarcastic tone, somewhat irritated by my last comment. *"You're just as ill as I am. Tell me about your illness."*

"Well, I have schizophrenia. Most people think the term means multiple personalities, but that is a different disorder. The misconception arises because schizophrenia means 'split mind,' and people think that means a split personality. It's just a confusion of the terms.

"I actually have a subtype of schizophrenia called paranoid schizophrenia," I add. "All schizophrenias are illnesses that distort one's perceptions of reality. They are characterized mostly by psychotic episodes where you have a break from reality. Some of the symptoms are hallucinations, such as hearing voices. However, they can include seeing visions as well. Delusions are also very common. Usually, in cases like mine, you experience paranoid thinking where you imagine people are trying to harm you or kill you. Ironically, those are called 'positive symptoms,' because they are added to what a normal person would experience. Additionally, there's another set of symptoms, called 'negative symptoms,' which include loss of motivation, apathy, lack of socialization, decrease of enjoyment, etc. It's like being a zombie, but you're conscious the whole time. It's really boring."

I started becoming ill when I was about 19 years old, which is a typical onset for mental illness. The onset of most mental illnesses is between the ages of 18 and 25. With schizophrenia, men generally develop the disorder in their late teens and early 20s, and women generally develop the disorder in their late 20s and early 30s.

Although there are many movies about the fine line between genius and insanity, mental illness strikes people of all intelligence levels. It is found in all races and ethnicities throughout the world. While schizophrenia strikes 1 percent of the population, bipolar strikes 2 to 3 percent of the population. They are both quite common as illnesses go. They both are partially hereditary, but most people with them have no family history of the illnesses. It seems that the most common risk factor for developing severe and persistent mental illness is being human.

I take a sip of my vanilla latte. "I'm excited about becoming a writer," I say. "I finally have some sort of purpose and a future. I've been living so long without one, and I've been trying all sorts of different things. However, nothing seems to work. I fail at everything I try."

"Why do you think you keep failing?"

"Lots of different reasons," I pause to think, and then continue. "Last night, I realized the big reason why I fail: I've been having this hyperreligiosity. I have become so intense about my faith that I haven't been taking care of my own needs. I think that is why I keep failing at things, because I haven't been taking care of myself first. How am I going to be good at helping others if I can't take care of myself first?"

I paused to think again. "That's part of it," I say. "Another part of it is not having confidence in my own abilities anymore. I used to be so confident, even arrogant to the point where I believed I could achieve and succeed at anything. But since becoming ill, I don't have that confidence anymore. I suppose that is because when I got ill, I started trying different things and kept failing at everything."

I have tried to go back to school to finish up my college degree, but to no avail. I had to drop out yet again. I even tried going to a technical school to get a degree more quickly, but that effort fizzled out too.

My whole life I have been an overachiever, and now with the disability from my illness, I can't achieve anything. Consequently, I do feel like a loser. I haven't even been able to graduate from college, and my former friends are finishing up at

Oxford, Harvard, and the like. I am embarrassed at becoming only a shadow of a man. Now, however, with my new proposed career, I see a glimmer of hope that I will be able to accomplish something.

"I want a big project to work on," Benji says. *"I want an empire."*

"You're going to have one, I think, with your landscaping business."

I finish off my vanilla latte, but we continue chatting.

"It sucks," Benji says, *"because you feel like you just sit idle for a long time, and you see people your same age progress; it is like a long digression."*

"I'm trying to keep up hope. It is as if I had been away in the military for three years and I'm returning to normal life, trying to reestablish some purpose in my life. However, it has been over seven years now, and I still haven't started again. My dad said it was like I went off to war, but I didn't come back; I'm like a POW. Maybe I'll come back some day. What's funny about my dad's comparison is that when I took the MMPI test, the Minnesota Multifaceted Personality Inventory, I registered high for post-traumatic stress disorder, which is what soldiers get when they have experienced serious combat. I registered high because of my experiences with my illness. Psychologically, the two experiences are the same."

Chapter 3:
Early Symptoms

I am waiting for Benji outside Starbucks while smoking a Marlboro Red. I hate that I smoke. I never thought I would become a smoker, and no one else could have predicted that either, because I was always into sports and weight lifting. I, therefore, thought of my body as a temple. Even more so than that, I was a nerdy do-gooder, and so the thought of smoking never even crossed my mind. I began smoking when I was just starting to develop schizophrenia. I was a sophomore at Caltech, and one day I decided to go to the gas station to buy a pack of cigarettes and a lighter. I was dreadfully nervous when buying the pack, because I felt like I was doing something illegal. I then went back to my apartment, went out on the balcony, and had the first cigarette of my life. Surprisingly, I enjoyed it. Smoking a cigarette was better than drinking alcohol, because, unlike the extended buzz from alcohol, the cigarette only gave me a buzz for a couple of minutes. Consequently, I could have one cigarette and then get right back to work. Smoking cigarettes wasn't going to take up my whole night or make me sick the next day.

Every now and then I quit smoking, but it never lasts. The addiction is not what brings me back to the cigarettes. Instead, I do it because the nicotine helps reduce some of the symptoms of my schizophrenia. One way that it helps is to improve concentration. Every time I go for a period without smoking, I'm unable to concentrate at all. Furthermore, I wear a nicotine patch when I know I will not be able to smoke for an extended time, but even that doesn't help enough. A year ago I tried to quit smoking by using the patches: I managed only three days. I had to start again because my concentration was so poor that when I would think a sentence-length thought, I would forget the beginning of the thought by the time I got to the end. So I started smoking again, and now I can concentrate again.

All of these reflections dissipate as I see Benji approach. He isn't wearing a jacket. I ask him about it, and he says that it is warm. It is only about 30 degrees, and although I do like cool weather, I think we have seriously different ideas of what warm is. I leave it at that, and we walk into Starbucks.

The female barista Benji chatted with last time we were here is working again. She remembers that Benji drinks decaf, and she introduces herself to us. She is a cute young woman, and as she chats with us, I can tell she is interested in Benji. She isn't flirting with him, but she is speaking in an overly friendly way, even more friendly than what you would expect from a Starbucks barista. I don't meet friendly people very often in Minnesota, despite the whole "Minnesota nice" stereotype. I have met friendly people in Madison, Wis. for sure; but rarely in Minneapolis.

The barista serves our drinks, Benji's decaf caramel macchiato and my regular vanilla latte, and we grab a seat at a table near the back of the establishment. A bustling Tuesday afternoon at Starbucks means that the more comfortable places to sit are already occupied. We chat for a few minutes before I take out my tape recorder. I place it on the table, turn it on, and we begin:

"Benji and I are sitting in Starbucks at 50th and France having the second of our recorded conversations." I begin laughing about how geeky I feel in trying to document the occasion. Benji shoots me an "oh God" sort of look.

"All right," Benji says, wanting to get started.

"You mentioned last time," I say, "that you have bipolar disorder. What were the first symptoms that you can say you had? The first change from who you were before your illness?"

"I really noticed the first symptoms during my freshman year in college. The symptoms were kind of hidden, but I would experience long spells where my mood was completely different."

"How was it different?" I ask.

"My moods seemed to change each semester. Looking back at my transcript, my semesters go from on the honor roll, to off the honor roll, honor roll, far off the honor roll again. It seemed that every time I was happy, enjoying life, and gregarious, etc., I wouldn't make the honor roll because I wouldn't pay attention to school at all. On the other hand, when I was really depressed and didn't have any interaction with anyone, my grades went through the roof."

I had always heard that people were more productive when they were manic, so I want to clarify what he is saying. "So you were more productive when you were depressed rather than manic?"

"*Well, I spent my time alone and did homework,*" Benji says, then adds, "*and hated life.*"

"How were those initial symptoms different from when you were in high school?"

"*I was both gregarious and productive all the time.*"

"What were some of the first things," I begin, but change my question. "How long was that period, those swings in your grades?"

"*It occurred for three years.*"

"When you were in this more gregarious mode, what things were you doing?"

Benji answers matter-of-factly. "*Drinking a lot.*"

"Like at parties, not by yourself?"

"*No, not by myself, never by myself.*"

I begin to think about what I know about his college life. "You were in a fraternity, right?"

"*Yeah.*"

"So no one recognized any problem with you going to parties all the time."

"*Well,*" he says, "*I had so many different people I could go out drinking with that I could go out every night and be irresponsible.*"

Similar to Benji, I didn't recognize my first symptoms as symptoms either. Virtually always someone will go through a period, sometimes a significant period, where they are ill with a mental disorder and go undiagnosed.

CHAPTER 3: EARLY SYMPTOMS

"The first symptom I noticed," I say, "in hindsight, was social withdrawal. It started about eight years ago. I was at Caltech studying science, and I played on its Division III baseball team. During my sophomore year, I stopped playing baseball and stopped hanging out with my friends. I was popular at the time, because everyone at this school is really geeky. Since I was only moderately geeky in comparison, I was rather cool. Therefore, despite being popular, I stopped hanging out with my friends, stopped socializing, and isolated myself in my dorm room."

During the summer after my sophomore year, I participated in the Summer Undergraduate Research Fellowship (SURF) program at Caltech, doing research on chromium in groundwater. This program was a great opportunity to get hands-on research experience, but I quickly found that I didn't have the motivation to do the work. I barely made it into the lab that summer and clearly didn't put in the hours I should have. At the end of the summer, I was supposed to write a research paper stating my findings and to give a presentation outlining what I had done during the summer. I turned in the paper late, doing a half-ass job on it. Furthermore, I never showed up to present my findings. This was a drastic change from before, and I did notice it at the time. I could never understand why I had become so lazy, but I thought that perhaps it was because I was unhappy at Caltech.

A lot more went on with me during this period, but I usually don't tell people about it. I'm a very private person. I find it embarrassing that I'm so incredibly crazy, and so I keep my craziness to myself as much as possible. The first thing I learned about living with a severe and persistent mental illness is to always have a smile on your face and to never tell anyone about your symptoms. That's how I get by among normal people at least. I intentionally confuse people into thinking that I'm healthier than I am, and I can do this fairly well since I'm high functioning for someone with schizophrenia. This pretense sometimes backfires though, because people don't understand why I may not be able to live up to life's expectations, and so I receive no sympathy and usually some level of condemnation.

I ask Benji to tell me more about what happened after the swings in his grades. He begins, *"I'd say the breaking point, the trigger point, that exposed my bipolar disorder was when my grandpa passed away from a stroke. I was pretty close to him, and they say traumatic events can be triggers. For six months after his death, I was completely reckless, over the top, and not focusing on school. I would pull it together at the last minute, doing all-nighters at the end of the semester just to pass classes with low Cs."*

"What did your parents think?" I ask. "Did they see your sliding grades?"

"They were supportive. They'd say, 'Try harder.'"

"They didn't suspect something was wrong?"

"No. During this whole time, I had this ongoing conversation with my parents where I'd be really good, and I wouldn't call them for months. Nevertheless, they would leave me messages all the time. I would maybe return a phone call every couple weeks, and they'd figure I was doing fine. However, during the months when I was

depressed, I would call them almost every day. I had no one to talk to about everything that was happening and about how bad I felt about everything. A lot of my depression I blamed on the pressure I put on myself to try to find myself. I couldn't find the right majors, something like that. My parents thought I was just searching for myself, too."

I get a bit excited. "I did the same thing with the majors, constantly switching them."

"I wanted to be an investment banker and do something in high finance. Now though, I don't have the ability to cope with the stress involved in a job like that. I say that because I would be continuously coping, having only the monetary compensation to keep me afloat with happiness. Now, I'm choosing to study something I find more interesting but with less monetary compensation, and I'm fine with that now. I was always measuring myself to my father and was thinking that I had to be as successful or more. Of course, that need is pretty common with a lot of people, that complex of having to measure up to your dad. No one wants to take a step down in class. Consequently, I think a lot of that pressure to succeed perpetuated my disorder."

"Did you come up with some huge business plans?" I ask.

"Yeah," Benji says, *"I didn't want to work a day of my life for someone else. Therefore, my goal was to start my own company before graduating. It didn't happen, but I tried multiple times. The ideas I had for new businesses aren't that important, but the mental process of continuously having the delusions that I could do grandiose things created problems."*

I try to clarify. "The point is that these are huge dreams."

"These were dreams of billion-dollar companies that I wanted to create overnight. Realistically, things like that happen over the course of years and require many people's input. I realize now that I must learn to be content with lesser expectations."

"I find that true with me too," I say, realizing that Benji has just hit on the biggest change that I'm dealing with in my life.

I've had a tough time dealing with my lowered potential, and I believe that is what has caused suicidal thoughts in me over the years. Of course everyone has limitations, and I had them before I got sick as well. However, most people can't blame a lowering in potential on a particular cause, and so they have nothing to rage against. I, however, can and do blame my illness for this undesirable change.

Before I was ill, I knew that I would never be a professional athlete. God simply hadn't given me the necessary talents. I knew that from a young age, and I never felt bad about that. It seems that I suffer only when something I thought possible has become impossible. Perhaps it would be more accurate to say that a dream I felt entitled to has been deferred.

I ask Benji, "How do you tell the difference between a normal dream and a grandiose dream?"

"I still don't know."

"Still don't know? Can't tell?"

"I wish I could," he says. *"That's why I only dream small now."*

"Just do it step by step."

"Yeah. Now I take all my dreams one step at a time, like getting

a summer job, or getting a first job after finishing technical school, which is where I find myself. Although I still have grandiose dreams, I don't act on them. I think the medicine keeps me balanced enough, especially the antipsychotics. They keep me from going into a psychotic state where I believe my own delusions. So maybe I still have delusions from time to time, but I will only go for a day or two thinking about one before I realize that it is probably not a good idea."

"These are all grandiose delusions," I say, "as opposed to me with the paranoid delusions."

"Yep," Benji says. There is a lull in the conversation, and he asks me to tell him more about what happened with me.

"I feel very uncomfortable talking about this out loud," I say. "It is so personal or something. I do give speeches where I tell my story, but this is different for some reason. It feels weird."

Benji nods, and I know that since he shared his very personal stories, I will have to share mine. I begin again, this time more quietly so as not to be overheard by the other patrons. "First, I stopped socializing with people. Then, I stopped having motivation to do my course work and stuff like that. These changes in character are called the prodrome. They lead up to the first psychotic episode. I ended up being very unhappy at Caltech, so I transferred to the University of Wisconsin-Madison."

I chose Madison for several reasons. It was a decent university that I could easily get into, and it had tuition reciprocity with Minnesota, so it wouldn't be as expensive as Caltech. The strongest reason, however, was that all my friends from high school attended that university.

"Unfortunately," I say, "I couldn't get in until the spring semester, so I spent the fall semester of my junior year at home in Minnesota. While home, I decided I wanted to be a writer. So I would journal all day, every day. I would go to this Starbucks to journal, but I started to believe that spies had placed cameras on the ceiling to read what I was journaling, to get inside my head or something. This upset me terribly, but I didn't tell anyone. I immediately sort of escaped this by transferring to Madison. But there was no escape. At Wisconsin, I started to believe the CIA was after me, and I was being followed and monitored at all times. I even tore my apartment apart once looking for electronic listening devices that the CIA had planted. I also thought everyone I came into contact with was in on this conspiracy against me. It was quite frightening—terrifying all the time. After a year of Madison, I transferred to Iowa State University in Ames, Iowa, where my sister lived. While at Iowa State, I thought more spies were after me. This time they weren't CIA agents; they were, instead, former Soviet communists. They followed and monitored me, all the same stuff as before. This experience was quite terrifying, too. I thought they were going to try to kill me. That is how the paranoia started. It lasted three years total."

What I've just revealed is the boiled-down, sterilized version, but I don't want to talk about anything more personal than that out loud, at least not right now. The truth is that I became increasingly paranoid and delusional for three years. The first paranoid thought I had was during the summer after my sophomore year at Caltech. I had moved off campus into my own apartment, and I started to believe my neighbor was monitoring my comings and goings. I didn't make much of it at the time; I just thought he was some sort of pervert. I don't know why I started thinking this, but it seemed that he was always standing in his doorway when I would come or go from my apartment.

My paranoia continued to grow once I came home to Minnesota. I started having a lot of arguments with my mother, because I was convinced that she was snooping through my room when I was out of the house journaling at Starbucks. This paranoia grew into delusions, like thinking spies had placed cameras on the ceiling to read my journaling. Somewhere in the midst of all this, I went to see *A Beautiful Mind*. I remember walking out of the theater thinking that Nash's life was similar to mine, except that he was crazy, and I was sane.

"Did you tell anyone this was happening?" Benji asks, pulling me back to the conversation.

"It's common not to tell," I say. "I had a reason not to tell. I thought that if the spies found out I knew what they were doing, they would alter their tactics and monitor me in ways I couldn't detect. Thus, I believed I could manage the situation if I kept my mouth shut and pretended nothing was happening. I couldn't tell my parents anything because they would probably slip up and let the spies know what was going on—and if they did that, it could put my family in danger as well."

"How were you doing in school?" Benji asks.

"My performance drastically changed. While this was happening, my grades were slipping. I went from having straight As and graduating tied for first in my class in high school to straight Fs and failing my classes in college. My parents never saw any of these grades because they stopped looking at my grades around the eighth grade—they were always As in everything. Since they never saw any of my college grades, they didn't know anything was wrong. The only thing they picked up on was that in California and later in Wisconsin, I never cashed any of the checks they sent me to pay for food and that sort of thing. I never cashed them because I didn't have any motivation to go to the bank. Although my dad thought that was weird, he thought it was because I was too busy doing school work."

I find myself worn out from this conversation. It's draining to confront my insanity. I certainly don't relive the experiences, but speaking of such personal events is tiring nonetheless. So I decide that is enough for today, and turn off the tape recorder. Benji and I finish our drinks and head out.

CHAPTER 4:
PSYCHOSIS AND MANIA

It has been snowing for the past couple days, which has resulted in a total of 14 inches of snow. Amazingly, the news media has been playing the snowstorm up as if we are all going to die from a few inches of snow. I don't remember snowstorms being so sensationalized on the television news when I was younger. Everyone seems to be an alarmist these days. I understand why they do it; some people will do anything to make a buck.

Snowstorms do affect my life. I have been having terrible anxiety about driving and riding in cars for the past two years or so. I keep envisioning myself crashing and becoming a quadriplegic. I thought this anxiety was premonitions from my illness, but last month when I told my doctor about these thought processes, he surprised me by stating that the anxieties were a result of my medications, not my disorder. I have the option to add an additional med to counteract the anxiety, but then I would have to deal with a whole other set of side effects.

Treating mental illness isn't like treating other illnesses. Even though mental illnesses are biological illnesses like any other, modern psychiatry is still in its infancy, and treatments are poorly understood. As such, the goal of treatment seems to be partially exchanging one set of symptoms, those from the illness, with a second set of symptoms, those from the medication. The goal is that life with this second set of symptoms (and some of the first set) will be more bearable than the first set.

I don't know whether I will add the extra med. Feeling so uncomfortable about driving has constrained what I can do, but I don't know if I can put up with more medication side effects. I'm on two different antipsychotics, and the one that helps the most in reducing my paranoia and hallucinations is the one causing both my weight gain and the anxiety. Thankfully, today Benji offered to pick me up and drive me to Starbucks. Usually, he drives us around town. Despite the stereotype about bipolar people driving recklessly, I find that my anxiety is the lowest when he drives. I trust his driving, but also, I trust the performance of his race car: a red Audi A4 that he got as a college graduation gift.

After he pulls into a parking spot in front of Starbucks, we make our way inside. I notice that Benji has gel in his hair, obviously trying to look good for the barista with whom we have been chatting every time we come here. We quickly notice that she isn't working today, so we get our drinks and head toward the back.

We don't begin recording immediately, because Benji has some big news to tell me. When he was in the shower this morning, he came up with a business idea, a new plan for his landscaping design career. We chat about it for a few minutes, and then he decides that he must call his dad to tell him the big news. They get into a conversation that lasts about 45 minutes, and as I sit waiting for the phone call to end, I realize that this might be exactly what he needs in his life. He has been trying so hard to achieve success, but each time he has an idea it is stymied by reality when he realizes that it is merely his grandiosity at work. However, this plan is different. From what I can tell, this plan isn't grandiose at all; instead, he has thoroughly and thoughtfully planned for his future. He is so excited that he can hardly sit still. I, too, become thrilled for him.

The call finally comes to an end, and Benji goes to order another drink. When he returns, we begin recording our conversation.

"We are sitting at Starbucks at 50th and France," I say. "This is the third of our recorded conversations about our lives." I point to the coffee table. "I see that you brought a marble-covered notebook with you today, Benji. What is that about?"

"*It is just where I keep all my grandiose ideas,*" he says.

"Didn't you buy a whole bunch of these notebooks or something?"

"*Well,*" he says, "*it's funny that you mention that. They were on backorder at the time I wanted to buy one. I was feeling extremely grandiose, so I decided to buy 20 of them instead of one.*"

"So you write down all your ventures and adventures in there?"

"*Yeah.*"

"I wanted to talk today a little bit about our experiences with psychosis," I say, "the nitty-gritty details. You said last time that the trigger that set your psychosis in motion was your grandfather's death, you experienced six months of off-the-wall behavior."

"I'll say. I had six months of grandiose delusions, but the psychosis itself probably didn't start until after that period. Only during the last month did I become completely psychotic."

"What did you do in that period?" I ask. "Were you manic at the time?

"*Yeah,*" he says. *"I'd go on probably two hours of sleep a night, and some nights I would get no sleep at all."*

"Did you feel tired when you didn't have any sleep?"

"No, never; I never felt tired." Benji continues. *"I drank a lot of coffee; I drank a lot of alcohol; I even drank a lot of coffee and alcohol at the same time. I remember one night where I brewed an entire pot of coffee, and I alternated between drinking one cup of coffee and one beer until I drank probably 16 cups of coffee and eight or nine beers."*

"Where were you at this time? Were you at home?"

"In my frat house."

"When my illness was just starting," I begin, "I went through a three-year period of increasingly worsening mental health, but the illness really started in earnest when I was going to school at Madison. I remember the very first incident occurred at a Starbucks there. I hung out every day at the Starbucks. While I was there one day, I decided that a middle-aged guy at the coffee shop was in the Secret Service. This year was the spring of 2002. 9/11 had happened the previous year, and the Conference of Mayors meeting was taking place in Madison. I suppose that all these things led me to believe that this guy was a Secret Service agent. From a few talks I had with him, I discovered that he was quite intelligent. So I was shocked to learn that he worked at a deli making sandwiches. This discovery upset me somehow because I was convinced there was no way this smart guy would work at such a menial job. Thus, I determined that he must be a Secret Service agent preparing for the Conference of Mayors. The conference would need tight security because the President was coming to speak. However, after the conference passed, he was still there. He came to Starbucks every day, and it didn't appear that he had a job. At this point, I started to believe he must be working for the CIA, and that he was there to spy on me. My plan was to befriend him. Consequently, I would have daily conversations with him. Trying to spread misinformation, I would pretend to have different beliefs than I actually had, like fictitious political and religious beliefs. I was spinning these lies to mislead this spy."

My fear of spies extended beyond Starbucks. I was certain my apartment was bugged. During this period, I used to talk aloud to myself a lot. To mislead the spies, I started to talk fake thoughts when I was in my apartment. I was also journaling a lot at this time. I would journal 10 to 20 pages a day, and because I thought the spies were reading these journals, I started writing fake journals, too. I would write pages and pages of thoughts that I didn't have, all in an effort to mislead the spies. I even started to think that the placement of books and newspapers on tables at the coffee shops were efforts of the spies to plant information into my brain. I thought that virtually every single person I came into contact with was in on this plot against me.

My paranoia was systematic in some regard. When I began thinking that the CIA was after me, I first believed that anyone who was older than college age could be an agent, for agents any younger than about 22 would be unlikely. I also knew that white men were probably overrepresented at the CIA. Therefore, older, white men were the first people I suspected of being in on a conspiracy against me. But then I realized that the CIA would also know that I knew this, and so I had to start suspecting more unlikely people. As a result, I started suspecting younger men and then minorities. I became even more suspicious of people who were black, because they would be the group least likely to be represented in the CIA. And then I suddenly realized my Achilles heal, so to speak. I was naturally least suspicious of women, especially beautiful, sweet ones. So I determined that the CIA would come after me through this weakness. As time passed and my paranoia grew, no one was trustworthy; everyone could be plotting against me.

Shockingly, while in this distrustful state, I started dating a woman I thought was working for the CIA. But the only reason I dated her was to further spread misinformation. The relationship only lasted about a month. I was suspicious of her the entire time we were together, and when the paranoia became too much and when I had no further use of her, I put an end to the relationship. During the summer after my first semester, I made a friend at Madison, my only friend. I thought he was working for the CIA too, and so I used our conversations to mislead the spies as well.

Although I thought he was working for the CIA, I really liked him, and he became my best friend. We would talk for hours on politics and philosophy, and by the end of the fall semester when I was set to transfer to Iowa State, I no longer believed that he worked for the CIA.

"Very interesting, Andrew," Benji says. *"Looking back at this time, when do you feel like you were completely psychotic?"*

"It's hard to say, because the psychosis built up slowly. Over a couple of years, I became increasingly psychotic."

"One significant difference between my collapse and yours is that I had a psychotic buildup that collapsed all at once and I needed to be hospitalized. But with your breakdown, you somehow escaped the hospital the whole way down."

"When I left Madison and went to Iowa State," I say, "things got a lot worse. I would say I was clearly psychotic at that time."

"For how long a period of time?"

"For a few months," I say. "That was the spring of 2003. I thought the Russians were after me to kill me."

I believed the Russians were after me because they thought I was working for the CIA. At first they did not want to kill me. They, instead, wanted me as a double agent. However, they soon learned I couldn't be turned against my own country. They then had no other recourse but to kill me.

I continue. "At first I thought they planned to kill me by poisoning my food, so, I locked myself in my dorm room. By this time, I was completely psychotic. I hadn't taken a shower in like a month. I wore the same clothes, and got planter's warts over the entire soles of my feet from wearing the same socks every day. Despite all of this, I survived. I even lived up to a week by eating only my garbage because I was certain I was being poisoned."

I had to wear the same clothes over and over again because I didn't have enough motivation to do my laundry. My lack of motivation even kept me from taking a shower. Surviving off my own garbage wasn't as extreme as it may sound. I had a huge mound of garbage in my dorm room because I couldn't throw anything away. Whenever I would get delivery food, the delivery place would print my name and address on the packaging. If I were to throw away the packaging, the spies could go through the dumpster to find out the places I got deliveries from and could poison my food before it reached me. Out of this huge mound of garbage, I found left-over scraps of food and condiment packets. One day I was elated because I had found horseradish sauce inside an Arby's bag.

I take a sip of my latte. "This transpired at the end of the semester. It all came to a head when my mother picked me up and took me home. My parents immediately took me to see a psychiatrist, but I didn't tell her anything. I lied to her, because I thought she was working for the communist spies, too. I should have been hospitalized right then, because I was a danger to myself and probably to others too. I was quite suicidal at the time."

I take a breather for a second, and Benji gives me a reassuring look. I have found that the more I talk about my illness the easier it gets, but I have never talked about my experiences with anyone in as much detail as today, and it isn't easy. What makes it difficult is the fear I have in describing both my experiences and my thought processes. I'm actually perfectly comfortable with everything I have been through, but I fear how others are going to react to what they hear. I'm slightly saddened to think that I won't ever trust anyone enough to relate my entire story.

"Benji," I ask, "how were you diagnosed?"

"This is what happened to me during my state of increasing psychosis," he begins. *"I was working on a grandiose business plan to start a venture capitalist firm that would specialize in the developing Asian markets."* He pauses, and then adds, *"Sounds complex."*

"It is complex," I say.

"This plan isn't something that I could have done with my expertise, with my studies in economics. However, due to my illness, I thought I could."

"Was this before or after you went to China?" I ask.

"After I visited China for the summer, I basically I wrote up this business proposal. I soon became increasingly paranoid where I would write up these contracts, contracts of . . ." he says, searching for the right word.

"Intellectual property?" I suggest.

"Yeah, intellectual property. I didn't have anyone sign them, but I was going to propose to all my friends that they sign these contracts which stated that anything I proposed to them was my intellectual

property, and they couldn't take it away from me."

"Did you show the contracts to any of your friends?"

"*No,*" Benji says. "*The only person I showed a contract to was a professor. I was taking business law at the time and I decided to seek the help of my professor to write a contract for my intellectual property rights. I think he could tell I was becoming increasingly worse with my illness, but he couldn't do anything about it. I remember telling him that I was writing a screenplay, also. I had two ideas that I would entangle, and one idea would push the other. If you were to make a circle with two arrows on it, each arrow pushes the other around. I had the venture capital idea I was trying to create, while simultaneously recording and journaling everything that was happening to me. I planned to turn the journal entries into a documentary about my life, either about failing or succeeding in the venture. I was doing these two things at once—they perpetuated each other.*"

"Did he think what you were trying to do was a joke that a college student was planning, or did he take you seriously," I ask.

"*I'm not quite sure what he thought. Looking back on it, it is tough to tell because I was psychotic at the time.*"

"Did you type up these contracts, or did you write them out in crayon or what?"

"*I wrote the contracts in Sharpie marker in my journal, and I wrote a business proposal on one page of paper and printed it out over 100 times to hand it out to everyone. Basically, I took a simple economics theory of marginal utility. Most marginal utility curves are $Y=1/X$, where it is exponential decay. I took that where X would equal you, your parents, your family, or anything that could* *be exponentially larger. Then Y equals what you are trying to per-petuate yourself to be.*"

"That doesn't make any sense to me," I say.

"*No, it doesn't. It doesn't make any sense, and it shouldn't make any sense.*"

"But it made sense to you then."

"*Yeah,*" Benji says. "*So I had this idea that if I met with one person at a time and gave them my business idea, the X could get larger. The day these plans all came to a halt was when I went to explain my thesis or business plan to the dean of the business school, hoping he would help launch my idea. I waited outside his office for him to show up from 5 in the morning until 7.*"

"You hadn't slept, right?" I ask.

"*I hadn't slept in a week.*"

"How did you look?"

"*I was wearing a suit,*" Benji says. "*Maybe I didn't sleep in it, but I had dozed off a few times in it. I was in bad shape. I remember cutting my hair, which had grown too long, in front of a mirror with scissors that same morning—like they do in the movies.*"

"Oh, my gosh."

"*After* The Wall Street Journal *was delivered to his office, I took it out and went through it with a pen. I found a Lehman Brothers ad with different banks listed on it. I highlighted all the banks where I knew people who worked there. I was certain that they would give me a business loan for the venture capitalist endeavor. My plan was totally insane, because I also wrote all these names of people who were going to help me succeed. One name belonged to the director of* Sex in the City; *this person was going to direct my documentary. At the time, I was also failing a class in the history of economic theory. I was failing because every paper I wrote was completely out there. For example, I wrote my midterm paper on utopian socialism and how it relates to the movie* Easy Rider."

"What did the teacher say?" I ask. "What did you get on that paper? An F?"

"*No, that paper was my best grade. Usually I got Ds or Fs, but on that one I got a C-.*"

"Very creative."

"*Yeah,*" Benji says, "*I got a C- for creativity. I met with the professor, and I told him that I was going away for a while. I was planning to drop out of school at that time. I thought I was on the verge of failing, so my answer to the problem was to just drop out.*"

"Emotionally, you were still on the high?"

"*Yes. I was okay with being a college dropout. That was fine with me.*"

He pauses. "*How about you? With you, it wasn't a choice to drop out of school.*"

"I was failing everything," I say. "When I transferred to Iowa State, the first month or so I didn't have symptoms, and I thought I had escaped the spies. I was now studying electrical engineering, my fifth different major. Although the average test scores from the other students in the class were like 45 percent, 50 percent, I was getting 100 percent on all the tests. Then, suddenly, I thought the spies were after me. So I stopped going to class. I could ace the tests if I showed up, but I stopped taking them. Not surprisingly, I failed everything. I failed a library class where all you have to do was show up once, and they show you were the books are."

Benji gives a loud audible laugh, and I continue. "So it was pretty bad, and I failed out of school. I was okay with it too—but for different reasons than yours. I wasn't happy; I was very upset, sad, and suicidal at the time. The weight of the world was on my shoulders, because I was going to be killed by spies at any moment. I was so freaked out that I just wanted it to end, and I knew the only way it could end was to take my own life. Thankfully, when I left Iowa State for home, the psychiatrist gave me some meds. At first I thought they were poison, but I took them because I wanted to die. Then I started doing better, and suddenly these people weren't after me. I never received a diagnosis at the time. The psychiatrist said that they don't give diagnoses, they just treat the symptoms. However, that is a huge lie; they do give diagnoses."

"Did they tell your parents the diagnosis?" Benji asks.

"No, they couldn't talk to my parents because I was over 18. They wouldn't tell me because, I think in hindsight, it would have been too hard for me to handle, having that label. So I started going to school at the University of Minnesota the next fall, and I was doing so much better that I was getting As in my classes. I was happy, and that spring I met a woman. Well, I had gone off my meds around Christmas, because they were causing weight gain and because I thought I was cured. Suddenly, my symptoms came back. When I would return to my apartment at the U, I would have to search it for assassins; I thought they were hiding inside, waiting to kill me. I started to believe the bathroom fan was communicating messages to me. I also started hearing voices; they were just murmurs though, as if someone had left the radio on and it was tuned to a talk station. I even began to visually hallucinate. Mostly the hallucinations were benign things, like seeing rainbows on the walls and such. Not all of my hallucinations were benign though: Sometimes I would see demons and monsters with big jaws and sharp teeth that would come out of my ceiling and would chomp at me as I would lie in bed. I was awake when this was happening. I wasn't dreaming, and I truly believed the horror that I was seeing was real, and it was scaring the shit out of me. I told my girlfriend what was happening, and she convinced me to see a psychiatrist. This time I went to a new, better psychiatrist. After talking to him for an hour, he diagnosed me with paranoid schizophrenia. It had been four years since the first onset of my symptoms. That meeting occurred on Oct. 15, 2004. That day is when I got my diagnosis."

CHAPTER 5:
SOME THOUGHTS

I feel a little down today. Nothing has gotten any worse in my life, but still I feel a bit down.

Not long ago I caught a television program about a woman with terminal cancer. She was young and beautiful, and the show successfully tugged at my heartstrings. As I watched, I kept making little comparisons between her illness and mine—specifically how our illnesses interfere with our lives. By the end of the program I was convinced that I would rather have cancer than schizophrenia. Both are horrible, of course, but there is always an end to cancer: You either become a survivor or you die. In my thinking, either option is better than living a life with a persistent mental illness. Schizophrenia continues to rage on, and there is never an end in sight—unless of course you kill yourself, which, sadly, is all too common.

Much of the time my life feels like a living hell, and it is most unbearable when I start to believe that things won't ever improve and will likely become worse as my illness progresses. It is the doom-and-gloom prognosis hanging over my head that actually makes the present unbearable, because I replace thoughts of hope with thoughts of those dreadful statistics. Swapping hope for stats is something I do occasionally, and I usually only go without hope for a week or so at a time. In that week, however, I always become suicidal.

It isn't that I'm depressed during those periods of hopelessness. It is that the statistics are so horrible that I see no reason to live. They say that I won't have a career, a wife, or a family. These are the things that make life bearable, joyful, and meaningful. Without them, I feel as if there is no reason for me to be alive. However, when I'm doing something meaningful and working toward a goal, I'm happy and hopeful and not at all suicidal.

Presently, my life isn't objectively bad. Almost all my needs are met: I have a roof over my head, clothes to wear, and enough food to keep me fat. These are all necessary for survival, but I don't want to merely survive; I want to thrive. I suppose I'm asking too much and should be content as I am. In all honesty, I am quite content most of the time. But I still have dreams of great achievements and loving relationships. Those dreams of something better, something just beyond my grasp, will never be erased from my consciousness. They will always persist, and I will always strive. That is, of course, only while hope lives in my heart. During the weeks when the statistics blaze in my brain, my dreams vanish like fog being burned away by the sun in the early morning.

Similar to Benji, but not at all grandiose, I used to dream of huge businesses that I would start. I don't anymore, because I am forced to admit the disability caused by this illness would prevent me from starting such enterprises. But I used to think up business plans, and even as far back as high school I was interested in such matters: I was voted in the yearbook the most likely to run a Fortune 500 company. I actually thought I would be hugely successful, so becoming largely disabled is a great change for me. Nonetheless, I can still enjoy the ideas of business, even though I doubt I could ever work in such a field. What I like about business is the game. It is like chess, full of maneuvering yourself and outmaneuvering your opponent. Playing the game is what interests me about business, rather than the financial rewards that go along with doing a good job.

I find life to be very much like a game of sorts, and I think if you believe in a blissful, everlasting afterlife, then you can have a more removed perspective on life. Distancing yourself from life and taking it as it comes—or viewing life more like a game to be played rather than something quite serious—allows you to cope with setbacks and maintain a joyful demeanor despite adversity. I don't have this removed perspective all of the time, but when I do I'm happy. One caveat: I don't have other people depending on me to meet their needs. As a bachelor, it is easy to take it easy, but I would guess that as a married man with a family it might actually be quite difficult. I desperately want a family, but I fear that I couldn't handle the stress. If I ever get a family of my own, I doubt I would be able to hold onto that removed perspective.

I enjoy philosophy for similar reasons: It is a game of sorts, much like business or life. I simply love puzzling over problems. That is common among people with schizophrenia, and although it isn't a diagnostic symptom of the illness, it is a symptom that is frequently present. I spend hours and hours thinking up theories of my own, usually until the wee hours of the morning. The next day I try to tell my theories to whoever will listen, but they usually get a poor response.

My favorite time is during these late all-nighters. I don't seem to have as many deep thoughts as I did before becoming ill, and so when I have these periods of thoughts I have to relish them. My parents don't like it when I stay up late to philosophize. I think they see it as evidence that I'm sick, and they don't like the realization it brings up for them. It is as if they don't want to acknowledge my illness, and when they do, they try to use the past tense—"He was sick, and now he's doing better."

I enjoy late-night philosophizing because my brain is working like it did prior to me becoming ill. I'm thinking at a high level with all sorts of insights. It is enjoyable, and a bit nostalgic. During these times I don't think about my illness, and for a time I become my old self. That is what no one understands: I haven't been sick my entire life and I remember what it was like to be normal. I remember who I used to be.

Much of the time I long for my old self. But I tell myself that I'm better as who I am now, and in some ways, like my moral character, I am. In other ways, however, I'm not better, and that is hard to deal with. I do feel like I'm a different person now. And because my personality has changed so much (and my physical body—from being fit to being fat), others can't recognize me as that same person either. I used to think of myself as an unstoppable superstar. Now I feel like a loser.

CHAPTER 6:
GETTING DIAGNOSED

I climb out of my SUV, and I can see Benji through Starbucks' front window. I'm running a bit late because a friend of my mother's stopped over at the house, and I chatted with her a little too long. I hurry my way into the coffee shop.

Benji looks a little deflated, and I soon learn why; the friendly barista is not working this afternoon. We get our coffees and head toward the back. A few people are sitting at tables, but otherwise the place is almost empty. I'm able to get an armchair, and Benji gets the couch adjacent to it. We set our drinks on the coffee table, and I take out my recorder. I say I need a couple of minutes to relax before we start; the drive has made me a bit anxious. About five minutes pass, and just as we are about to start, an elderly woman chooses to sit at a table very near us. I'm worried that if she overhears our conversation about mental illness, she might become fearful. I have to record today, so I guess I will just have to take that chance.

"Today is..." I begin.

"*Monday*," Benji says.

"Today is Monday..."

"*Monday*," he says with emphasis. He is suddenly in a better mood than he was when I arrived here, and he is enjoying breaking up my attempt at meticulously documenting our conversation.

"Today," I say, "we are recording our fourth conversation. We are going to talk a little bit about the actual diagnoses, how they came about. So Benji, how did you end up in the psychiatrist's office?"

"*As I was saying, I was talking to my professor and dean at the time, and he gave me a card that read, 'Head Psychiatrist.' It had a name on it and a location on campus. I was told to go to this building that I had been to numerous times before to get cold medicine or what not. But on the way there I got lost, because I was completely disoriented, and I ended up sitting on a street curb crying uncontrollably. Someone asked me what was wrong, and I told him that I was lost.*"

"And this was on a campus where you had been like millions of times?" I ask.

"*Yeah, and it was my third year of school, so there is no reason I should be lost or crying uncontrollably. Strangely enough, I think I was crying because I was happy. I was mostly happy. But the person told me that I was right in front of the building I was supposed to enter. So I stood up and walked in. Once I got in the building . . . the dean had phoned ahead to tell them . . .*" Benji pauses, searching for the right words.

"To tell them you were coming?" I suggest.

"*To tell them I was coming and what my symptoms were*

and stuff. They told me to take a seat and then gave me a clip-board with a questionnaire, like a three-, four-, maybe a five-page questionnaire."

"What was on the questionnaire? Was it like a medical history you would get at a regular doctor's office?"

"*I don't know,*" Benji says. "*I didn't read it. Didn't read it, didn't fill it out. I couldn't focus enough to even think about filling it out. I tried to answer two or three questions about medical history and where I lived. I completely blanked out on where I lived. I didn't know my social security number and all that sort of stuff.*"

"How did you feel about that?" I ask.

"*It didn't matter at the time. I was so focused on starting my venture capitalist firm. Instead of concentrating on the questions, I was dreaming in my head what the business was going to be, and how my life was going to change because of it. I felt I was on the brink of genius. It was like stars up in the air, twirling around my head. Therefore, everything else was nonexistent to me. One thing I do remember is that, well, I was making a . . .*" he pauses, again searching for the right words.

"A documentary about your life," I say.

"*Yeah, I was making a documentary about my life and experi-ences. I thought the clipboard would make a good memento for my documentary, so I put it in my backpack. I stole the clipboard with the questionnaire.*"

"Do you still have it?

"*Yeah, I threw the questionnaire away when I got home, but I still have the clipboard with the pen and the curly cord at home. Another thing I remember was being drawn to this a wall with dif-*

ferent brochures. There were pamphlets for every different illness you could have mentally, maybe 15, 20 different color pamphlets that were each about five pages long. I grabbed one pamphlet of each and put them in my backpack, thinking I would need them. There was no reason to pick up all of the pamphlets, but I stuffed them in my backpack like they were important. I thought it might be a nice trinket to piece together my day because I didn't have a camera on me. My collapse into this disease was all really sudden for me. Everything crescendoed on one day."

Benji motions toward me. *"But with you, everything happened more slowly. What was the day like when you actually got your diagnosis?"*

"What was going on with me?" I ask.

"What prompted you into the doctor's office?"

"Well, I mentioned that when I was going back to school at the U of M, I was doing well. I had met a woman and things were going great, but then my symptoms started to return. My girlfriend convinced me to see a psychiatrist again, and I took her advice."

When I came home from Iowa State, the psychiatrist I saw was the first doctor to put me on medication. Because I thought she was a Russian spy, I transferred to a new psychiatrist after only a couple appointments. The second psychiatrist treated me for about six months or so, from mid-summer to mid-winter, but then I went off my medications and stopped seeing him, too. This second psychiatrist was the doctor I started seeing again when my girlfriend prompted me to seek treatment.

I pause to take a drink of my latte. "He immediately put me

back on a low dose of medication, but I realized this guy wasn't the right doctor for me. He wouldn't give me a diagnosis, and that made me mad."

It is actually required to give a diagnosis to bill the insurance company, and the diagnosis I was labeled with was "psychotic disorder, not otherwise specified." That label is pretty much a catch-all, meaningless diagnosis, and I knew that. I wanted my real diagnosis.

"I was convinced that I had schizophrenia, but he told me that people with schizophrenia should be put on a high dose of antipsychotic medication and written off as a lost cause."

This was the same doctor my parents talked to about the suicidal thoughts I was having during the summer after I left Iowa State. My parents wanted him to help me deal with my suicidal thoughts, to save me from killing myself. His response was simple: He couldn't save them all.

This psychiatrist was convinced that I didn't have schizophrenia, precisely because I thought I had schizophrenia. Apparently, if you think you have it, you must not have it. This philosophy must be the old catch-22 of the psychiatry world.

I continue. "I was really mad at him and transferred to a new psychiatrist. During my first meeting with my new psychiatrist, I had been on meds for about two weeks, not a high-enough dosage to take care of my symptoms, but I was pretty stable.

Although I wasn't psychotic at the time, I was still having delusions and hallucinations. The appointment was like a typical doctor's appointment. I waited outside, and then we went into a room and sat down in chairs. The stereotypical couch was not there, and I didn't have to lie down and tell my deepest, darkest feelings or anything. My parents were there with me as well."

The psychiatrist asked me if it were all right if my parents went into the meeting, and I consented. I was slightly apprehensive about that, for I had intentionally told them very little of what had been going on with me. I have never had a very open relationship with my parents, but the main reason why I hadn't told them about my experiences was because I didn't feel they were ready to hear about them. My father was still in denial, and I thought my mother too fragile to handle hearing about all that I had experienced. After my new psychiatrist made any suggestion, he always followed it with a question in a soothing voice—"Would that be okay with you?"

I take another drink and continue. "I basically recounted to him the history of what I believed to be my symptoms at the time. After talking for half an hour, midway through the appointment, my parents left the room. I then told my psychiatrist some more about what was happening with me. After another half hour, I received my diagnosis. He asked me a lot of questions, but he didn't ask me to explain any old proverbs. A common approach for psychiatrists to determine schizophrenia is to ask you to explain the meaning of a proverb. For example, they often ask what the following proverb means: 'People in glass houses shouldn't throw stones.' A person with schizophrenia will have difficulty explaining the meaning correctly because he or she will have trouble with abstract reasoning and give concrete answers such as 'because you will break the windows.' Answering incorrectly suggests that schizophrenia is the illness. I was pleasantly surprised when this doctor did not ask me anything like that. Dressed unassumingly in a sport coat and a tie, he was very nice. Talking to him was like talking to a normal guy. He really put me at ease."

I take a drink of my latte, and ask Benji, "What was your appointment like?"

"It was like a crash appointment, almost like an emergency appointment," he says. *"Everything in the office stopped because I had to come in and get diagnosed and be told to leave campus. I was in no shape to be on campus. It was basically a set up to get a medical withdrawal and to be sent off campus as soon as possible. They brought me into a room with this younger man, who was in maybe his early 30s and working for the main doctor who was overseeing everything. He was pretty inexperienced, I would say. My symptoms were so inflated at the time."*

"So obvious," I add.

"Yeah, I think he was quiet because he was really nervous. Mostly, he only saw people with anxiety and test problems and stuff like that. So he grabbed the thickest book he could from his bookshelf, like the bible of all things mental disordered."

"The DSM-IV," I say, "the Diagnostic and Statistical Manual."

"It was a big brown book. He flipped to a page, and, pointing to

a list of symptoms, he read them off as we looked at them together. He reads things like, 'Decreased need for sleep,' and I said, 'Yes.' Then 'Fidgety and pacing,' and I said, 'Yes,' and he kept going on with these different scenarios. I could go on forever on the list of what he asked, and I said yes to just about every question—about 95 percent of what he asked. And he said, 'Yes, you have manic depression or bipolar.'"

"When you were told that, what did you think? Were you in shock?"

"For me at the time," Benji says, *"it was great, because I was in the midst of making this documentary about my life, and being bipolar made my story all that much better. Going to the doctor's office and getting diagnosed with a bipolar disorder created a complete sensation that would add excitement to my story. On one level, my story was like a clueless guy who was starting a make-believe business, but now they are telling me I'm completely psychotic—or in the midst of psychosis, to be more precise. And so I'm thinking this is great, maybe I'm on the verge of the next* Beautiful Mind *movie."*

"What did you know about mental illness before that?" I ask.

"Nothing."

"Nothing?"

"Well, I knew some stuff," he says. *"I actually knew two friends who had the same disorder, but neither took his meds. One functioned all right and was just moody. The other slept a lot and had a complete lack of motivation. He kept failing out of school, or at least failing classes and taking medical withdrawals. But he would come*

back, only to take another medical withdrawal. I was told that I was failing all my classes except for one, and because of my illness I was, therefore, getting a medical withdrawal. I thought that was great, because my parents weren't going to know I failed all my classes. Furthermore, I felt like I was cheating the system or something."

"That made you feel even better?" I ask.

"I felt great. From there, I was escorted by my fraternity adviser to the local airport. A private jet picked me up and flew me home. My parents were freaked out."

"I can understand that."

"My dad's company has two jets, and they flew one down immediately to pick me up instead of booking a commercial flight. So that was sensational too, because I got to have a private jet pick me up."

Benji looks a little worn out from the conversation, but I don't know if it is as hard on him recounting such stories as it is for me. He then asks, *"For you, Andrew, was it a shock receiving your diagnosis?"*

"For me," I say, "it wasn't. Before I went to my current doctor, I went to the bad doctor, who told me people with schizophrenia are lost causes, and before him, I went to my first doctor, who I thought was the Russian spy. But right before I went to see my very first psychiatrist, I realized at some level that I had a mental illness. I looked online at the DSM list of symptoms, and I was convinced I had schizophrenia. I thought that right after I left Iowa State. I reasoned that since I left school, no spies should care to be after me anymore. After all, I was a dropout—a failure. I originally thought the CIA was after me because they wanted me as an agent, and then the Russians were after me because they thought I was working for the CIA. But now, it was pretty clear that I would not be doing anything with my life: I was just this loser. And so I went home, but nothing stopped. The paranoia was still there. This time I thought I would be framed for the assassination of a prominent political figure. And then I reasoned that the only way this could be happening to me, to be losing this game of intrigue, was if I were crazy. Finally, I went online and looked at the list of symptoms and diagnosed myself to have schizophrenia."

I have actually read that there have been other people who have diagnosed themselves with schizophrenia before the psychiatrists have done so, but from what I gather, this is very rare.

I continue. "Now this self-diagnosis occurred simultaneously with my belief that the paranoia was all true and happening. I had these two opposite ideas and I held both to be true at the same time. You can't explain it. It is just crazy. I thought I was sick, and, at the same time, I thought the psychiatrist was a Russian spy. This part of my illness is so complex that it is hard to explain. I think they call it 'schizophrenic thought,' to have two opposite ideas held to be true at the same time in your head. Therefore, to be finally told by a doctor that I had schizophrenia was not a shock. As I went along with treatment with my second psychiatrist, I was sure I had this illness because I had read all about it. Then when I got the diagnosis, I was relieved. I knew what I was up against and had something to fight against. Before, I didn't know what was going on with me. I was really relieved to have the diagnosis. Instead of being in denial, I was actually happy to get it."

That is not to say I was happy at the time. I was miserable. I had heard all about the dreaded prognosis associated with schizophrenia. I would be severely disabled, if not now then soon. I would never have a life worth living, and my suicidal thoughts persisted. But I was also relieved to have the diagnosis for another reason as well. My lack of motivation could be attributed to the illness. Even though I had thought that I had schizophrenia and had known there was a lack of motivation associated with it, it was a relief that others could finally view my lack of motivation as a symptom of my illness instead of a character flaw.

"So it didn't come as a shock at all?" Benji asks.
"Not at all."
"Did it mean that you wanted to seek help for it?"
"Yeah," I say, "that is a good thing. If they had told me I had it, and I had not believed them, I wouldn't be in treatment. So it was good I learned I had it before they did, or at least before they told me." I finish off my latte. "I'm wondering, Benji, what were the next steps for you. What happened after you got home?"
"Basically, they sent me away from school with a whole array of antipsychotic medicine, and I was a walking zombie for two weeks. I did nothing but lie on the couch, write in my journal constantly when I was awake, and then lie on the couch some more. I'd sleep probably 16 hours at night, and nap during the day. The little time I was awake was only like four to six hours. I was miserable. Then I

got an appointment with a doctor. I intensely remember the doctor's office, because it was built in a round circle and every doctor had a different colored door. The doctor came out to get me, and when I walked to his office, his was the one with the magenta pink door. I thought, 'Why do I have to get the doctor with the pink door?' He wanted to put me on straight lithium. He put me on a pretty high dose of it, but it didn't work for me."

Benji continues. *"By the second or third meeting with him, I was frustrated with my sedation and my lack of drive. I wasn't depressed, just had a lack of drive. I remember watching the movie* Garden State, *which is about a boy on a bunch of sedating meds. I don't know if he's depressed or what, but he goes off his meds. I didn't want to go off the meds—I just wanted to overcome them. So I stayed up all night watching the movie three times. Then I woke up early in the morning and went to my favorite restaurant, Mickey's Diner in St. Paul. I continued to write in my notebook about what I was going to ask my doctor. I had all kinds of questions about my illness, and he hadn't taught me anything. He just labeled me and wrote me off with medicine in eight minutes. My appointments with him were only eight minutes long."*

Benji pauses for a drink. *"While on my way to see him once, I was in the front seat of my father's Escalade, and I had a stack of Post-It notes. I was writing on the Post-It notes and would stick them on the dash. By the time we were on the freeway close to the exit, I had 20 to 30 Post-It notes on the dash. My dad asked, 'What are you doing? What are you doing?!' But my mom said, 'Let him be. He's going to the doctor and things are going to be better.' I wanted fresh air, so I opened the window, and all the Post-It notes blew out the window onto the freeway like snowflakes. I thought it was neat to watch, but I was completely upset because they were all my brilliant thoughts I had come up with to ask my doctor. So the ones that didn't go out the window I frantically grasped and then put them in my pocket. When I got there, I had all these Post-It notes I was shuffling in my hands. During the session with the doctor, I tried to ask questions, but he didn't want to answer any of them. Finally, I said, 'Can I just ask you one question?' And he replied in this authoritative voice, 'You can either listen to me, or you can go to the hospital.' I turned to him and said, 'I would rather go to the hospital than ever listen to you again.'*

"So you got rid of him," I say.

"*Yeah,*" Benji says. "*Right after that I said, 'You're fired,' like Donald Trump. I don't think he had ever been fired like that before. Maybe he had. But I walked out of the office in the middle of my appointment. Then he ran up to my parents and told my father I need to be taken to the hospital in the region with the best mental health facility. I got lucky enough to land in a great hospital where I got excellent treatment.*"

Chapter 7:
Hospitalization

I wasn't planning to meet Benji today, but he just called to say he is coming to pick me up. It is about 11 in the morning, but I haven't even taken a shower yet. Taking a shower is always difficult for me. It is hard to explain, but I think it comes from my lack of motivation. It involves a lot of effort and cannot be cut into smaller, more manageable pieces. I try to shower at least every other day, but often it is more like once every three days. I feel better on days I take a shower and am more likely to go out of the house for coffee. But I've noticed that it doesn't get easier; each time I get into the shower it is just as difficult as the previous time—it all depends on the degree of lack of motivation the illness is causing. A couple of years ago when my negative symptoms were really bad, I would only shower once every five or six days. I don't even want to think about how rarely I brushed my teeth.

Benji arrives, and he drives us to 50th. I don't like that I'm going out of the house without having showered, but I just did it yesterday, so I feel it will be okay. We walk into Starbucks and see that our barista is working today. Her pleasantries bring a smile to our faces. We chat with her as we order and wait for our drinks. Benji has switched from his caramel macchiato to plain decaf coffee, because he has put himself on a new budget plan to save money. Due to his illness, he sometimes buys expensive items that he neither needs nor can afford, and I hope this new plan will help prevent such purchases. It seems to be working.

Starbucks is busy today, and we are lucky to find a spot at a table. I pull out my recorder, and we begin.

"Today," I say, "we are having our fifth conversation. Benji, you said you were hospitalized for your illness, and today I would like to know a little bit about what that experience was like. How did that start? Did your parents drive you there?"

"*Well, as I was telling you before, I fired my psychiatrist, and he immediately recommended that I check into a hospital. I had to admit myself into the hospital voluntarily, so I agreed to go to the one recommended by my doctor. Members of the hospital staff brought me into this waiting room. I remember everything that happened vividly. For some reason, I had this glass—no, not glass—but plastic cube in my hands.*"

"Okay," I say.

"*And I kept folding these little paper boats that were going to represent my dreams. I would also write on these paper boats. The whole thing was . . .*" he pauses. "*Previously I had spent $2,000 on a party I gave at school, and I remember I bought about $400 or $500 worth of T-shirts so I could have my life slogan printed on them.*"

"What was the slogan?" I ask.

"*The slogan was 'Commitment to Excellence—Every Day in Everything I Do.' The whole idea was almost hubris—very arrogant, but it meant doing the best or better than anyone else in anything you've ever done. That was how I felt about myself. I believed that anything I touched would be better than anything anyone had ever done in the history of mankind. I was wearing one of these T-shirts and* Sponge Bob *pants in the hospital.*"

"Were they your pants, or did they give you pants?"

"*I had no clothes,*" Benji says. "*When I left school, I only had the clothes I was wearing. So I went to a local department store and my mom bought cheap clothes for me to wear until I could get my wardrobe from school. But anyway, I'm in the waiting room pacing and pacing and pacing in these silly clothes, and my mom pleads, 'Just sit down, please. Sit down.' I'm making a scene, which caused everybody to watch me. And then I say, 'Mom, do you know the only way to get the sailboats out of the plastic cube?' And she responds, 'What is it?' I answer, 'You have to break it!' And I throw it on the floor, causing the plastic cube to break into all these little pieces.*"

"Was this the emergency waiting room you were in?" I ask.

"*Yeah, the emergency waiting room. Then after a half an hour or 40 minutes, they help me. They take me in a wheelchair and wheel me up to Unit 47. The whole hospital is set up with all these different units, obviously, but for me, this was my unit and it was magical.*"

"Was that because 47 is a prime number?"

"*I don't know,*" Benji says. "*I had been counting prime numbers. I was curious about prime numbers. I think what I was interested in was that . . .*" He pauses. "*Forty-seven was a locked-down unit, and it was called the IBM program. That tickled me. They had this huge board, and it was color coordinated, with the whole schedule for the day. It said IBM across it, and I felt like I was stuck in the book 1984 where I was part of this planned community. The experience also was sort of like being in the movie* One Flew over the Cuckoo's Nest. *Since 47 was a locked unit, as soon as I got in, everything was taken away from me. I was very upset that they took my iPod because I had been doing nothing but listening to music over and over on it. At the other end of the unit was another door with a keypad; that was Unit 48. Another thing I was doing during this time with numbers was moving them around in my head to make new numbers, so I changed Unit 48 to Unit 84. I wanted to get over there because I thought there I would get my freedom."*

"That's 84 from the book *1984*?" I ask.

"*Absolutely,*" Benji says. "*That was the beginning of my stay at the hospital. Next, I was swifted into a room with one of the intake psychiatrists, and he drilled me with questions for about half an hour.*"

"Was that to rediagnose you?"

"*Kind of. And to see what state of psychosis I was in at the time, and what kind of timeline would be recommended for me.*"

"How long did you end up staying there?" I ask.

"*I ended up staying 19 days, which is funny because most patients don't stay longer than three to five days.*"

"I didn't know that."

"*Most people's insurance doesn't pay for more than three days. The commitment you sign in for is three days, so after three days you can sign yourself out. I guess I had the opportunity to do that at any time, but my nurses kept telling me not to, because they knew I wasn't well enough and that my insurance was good. My parents were willing to pay on top of that too."*

"What was a typical day like?" I ask.

"*At 9 a.m.,*" Benji begins, "*breakfast started. The whole experience was kind of like a game. How should I describe this? It is almost like the game of Life or Risk. There was constantly a little play going on between the patients and the practitioners, because you didn't know what your boundaries were. They aren't told to you, and you don't know what you are supposed to do during the day, except that there are certain times blocked off for activities you are supposed to go to.*"

"What were some of the activities?"

He continues. "*You don't have to go to the activities if you choose not to go. But to get privileges, you have to go to the activities. One was called music therapy. That was my favorite. We would go into an atrium room at the end of the unit. It was filled with plants and had a piano and a ping-pong table they could roll out. However, the most interesting part of this room was that it had well over 1,000 LP records that you could pull out of these crates and play during music therapy. The first night they had music therapy, I pulled out the Beatles'* Abbey Road *album. I played the whole album from beginning to end. Since I was completely delusional and spaced out at the time, it was the most amazing musical journey I had been on. There was a woman there with the same illness as I have. She is kind of a perennial patient, where every few months she has to come back for a week or two weeks.*"

"They call them 'frequent fliers,'" I say.

"*Yeah, frequent fliers. There were a bunch of women in there painting their nails, because that is what they chose to do during this time. You could do whatever you wanted. It was sort of free time. She asked to paint my nails, and I said, 'Sure.' So as my parents are leaving, I have my hands on the ping pong table, and these weird ladies are painting my nails. My parents didn't know what kind of place they were leaving me in. Understandably, they were nervous.*"

Benji takes a sip of his coffee, and continues. "*Another activity was recreational therapy. That was usually in the morning, right after breakfast. I remember that there was this rendition of* Somewhere Over the Rainbow *we would listen to every morning. It was kind of a reggae version of it.*"

"Was it Hawaiian?

"*Yeah.*"

"I have it at home," I say.

"*We'd listen to it and do yoga stretches. That was one of them. Another thing we had was . . . I forget the abbreviation, but it was basically craft time. We could color or build, or we could do papier-mâché. I remember that also was interesting, because the woman who ran it was named Andrea, and I asked her if I can call her Dr. Dre because she goes by Dre.*"

Benji lets out a laugh. "*At mealtime people were often upset because they didn't get the food they wanted. You slowly learn as they switch your meds, and you become more and more adapted to reality: Things become clear and more boring—more like real life. At the beginning of your stay in the hospital, everything starts out surreal. You think it is a game where you are in this weird system, but then you realize you are in the hospital, and things are more normal. To choose what you wanted for breakfast, you had to circle on your placemat what you wanted for the next meal. You could circle cereal: Rice Crispies or raisin bran. Then if you wanted two boxes, you could write 'times two' next to it. You could also choose pancakes, sausage and eggs, or both. You could write 'times two' next to these choices, too. No matter what you chose, that is what they would bring to you. Some people would do 'times two' to everything, and they would have two trays of food. They always told us we needed to fill out our menus, but for the first five days, I had no idea what they were talking about. I couldn't comprehend what that meant."*

"What were the other patients like in the hospital?" I ask.

"Well, everyone was at different levels of their illness. The first night I got there I was blown away because everyone was so unique and interesting. Being among these people was like being in a show, and I felt like I was trapped in a movie. That is what I told myself. I went up to two older gentlemen, and I asked them what I needed to do to get out of here. And they said it was like Star Wars, *and I had to use the force. They said, 'Things move without your own doing, and you just have to be calm and let things move and not worry about moving them back.' I learned what they meant by this right away, because I would start a puzzle. Then all of a sudden, the puzzle would be moved away and be back on the shelf. I would demand, 'Where's my damn puzzle?' Things like that. You'd be coloring with a bunch of crayons and paper one moment, and the next moment, the crayons and paper would be gone. Because I was kind of paranoid, I kept blaming my RN for doing things to me. I remember even as I was going into the hospital, I thought my dad*

had stolen my checkbook, but I had just misplaced it. While in the hospital, I accused the nurses of taking my stuff and not letting me have my iPod. The staff didn't want me to have my iPod because they didn't want someone to steal it. In reality, the people who moved things were the patients. I remember the first night that I slept there I went to my bedroom . . ."

"Did you have your own bedroom?" I ask.

"No, I shared it with multiple people because so many people came in and out. But when I went into my bedroom, there was a well-done piece of art drawn with colored pencil under my pillow. I never got to meet the person, but I think it was someone who left the night I came in. I'm guessing it might have been one of the older gentlemen, the one who told me to use the force. I called him Obi-Wan Kenobi, because he seemed like the character. I held on to that piece of art because I thought it was really interesting."

"Would you tell me more about these people you met?"

"They were interesting," Benji says. *"A lot of people were having similar delusions to me. I'd say about 70 percent of the people were having religious delusions where they thought things like the world was going to end soon. I was in the hospital when the tsunami hit Southeast Asia, and everyone thought this was like a great flood. We were watching it on CNN, and people were getting the wrong idea, claiming the apocalypse was going to come. There was one kid, whose name was Muhammad Ali—at least that is what we called him; I don't know his real name—who was from . . ."*

I can tell he is drawing a blank. "Somalia?" I suggest.

"Yeah, and he had these webbed fingers. He would hold up his hands and touch people, and they thought they were getting healed

by him. I don't know what his issue was, but he could hardly communicate and was heavily medicated. He even drooled. He was sort of like the real Muhammad Ali is today. Despite these complications, this kid could speak in his native language just fine. He kept getting all these phone calls. Family and friends could call the phone in the unit. Whenever it would ring, everyone would say, 'It is for Ali.' The calls were from his family. I guess he had a son in Seattle. I remember I gave Ali my T-shirt."

"The 'Commitment to Excellence' one?" I ask.

"*Yeah,*" Benji says, "*and he wore it the whole time in the hospital. He gave it back to me when I left. I remember he was so proud to be an American citizen, and he wanted a flag. He intensely wanted a flag. My mom had this little flag at home, and she gave it to him. He put it on a pencil and would wave it around as he would prance through the area.*"

He finishes off his drink. "*I met people with drug addictions. My hospital unit had a lot of people with cocaine and methamphetamine addictions.*"

"Did these patients have a dual diagnosis, or was the unit used for the mentally ill and the substance abusers."

"*Both. Sometimes they would find they had dual diagnosis, and other times they found that people with mania have similar symptoms to people with cocaine and methamphetamine addictions. So they told me it was tough to tell if people had mania or methamphetamine addictions when they would take them in. Therefore, these patients would be treated at the same place, at least initially, because this unit was like a holding area. From there, the doctors would work with social services to get them to other treatment centers. But back to the religious delusions, there was a time when people thought I was a prophet. I would walk around, and people would actually kiss my feet. All I have to say is that it was really weird, and I'm glad it is over."*

"What happened as you started getting better?" I ask.

"As I progressed and got better, drawing pictures, doing recreational therapy, and having music therapy seemed sort of childish. Therefore, I was moved to the other program, Unit 48, during the day."

"What did you do while you were in Unit 48?"

"That program had a different acronym, CPM, which stands for the Crisis Prevention Management program. For the most part, it was made up of people who were more . . ." Benji searches for the right words.

"High functioning?" I suggest.

"Higher functioning, yes, and less sick. Yet their symptoms were more acute. More of these people were just seriously depressed, and even more were suicidal. Unit 48 had less supervision because there was more trust. When I came to the first unit, the ratio of patients to nurses was two to one—two patients to every one nurse. Each patient almost had a personal nurse, which is almost unheard of. Then this other program, I don't know what the ratio was, but it was probably double, triple, or quadruple that ratio. The day at Unit 48 was spent in therapy."

"Like group therapy?"

"Yeah," he says, *"group therapy. I had to go to two different therapy meetings during the day. I hated that I ever asked to be moved to a different program, because it was just painful. I hated*

group therapy. For me, it was a waste of time. Some people get help from it, but with my disorder, it is not something that helps, I don't think. My disorder is not necessarily caused by my environment; it is biological. These sessions were geared more for people who had anxiety and depression that were triggered by events that occurred in their lives. After some time in this unit, I got even better and was moved to the least-supervised groups. That was Unit 39, which was on the floor below."

"How long did you stay there?"

"I think three or four nights. That place was boring. It was smaller, almost like a holding area. A lot of the patients were people going through medication changes, and they were worried about how they would react to them. They'd check into the hospital and stay there for three days or so, or just over the weekend, to see how they would do on a new medicine."

"They were trying to find the right medicines for you this whole time, right?" I ask.

"Every day I would see a psychiatrist. She was so comforting that I wish I could have stayed with her, but I couldn't."

"Did you ever get to see your parents?"

"There was visiting time every night from 6 to 8 p.m.," Benji says, *"and my parents came every day I was in the hospital."*

"That's nice," I say. "Did any of your friends from college come to visit? Or any other friends?"

"No, no one. I think they were all afraid."

"Does it still bother you today that they didn't visit?"

Benji pauses for a long time. It seems like a painful question. *"No, not really. A lot of people who come down with mental illness find themselves alone because others don't want to be around people with things they don't understand."*

CHAPTER 8:
NEXT STEPS

You would think that I should be happy that I have never been hospitalized for schizophrenia, but I don't find that to be the case. I'm in this middle ground where I don't fit in with people who are normal and I don't fit in with people with severe and persistent mental illnesses. Normal people think that I'm too mentally ill, and the mentally ill think I'm too normal. Of course, this feeling of being left out is a terribly stupid way to think. I know that, but I can't control feeling this way. I have been giving speeches around the Twin Cities to groups interested in hearing my story. Although I hear a lot of praise for my talks, at one, I overheard a woman say to the woman next to her, "Yeah, but he hasn't ever been hospitalized?" Is that a good enough reason to write off everything I had to say? But I suppose I'm terribly fortunate not to have been hospitalized, and so I will try to view it as a blessing.

Benji and I had planned to get together today at 4 in the afternoon, but I just received a call from him at half past 12, and he told me he's on his way over to pick me up. He wants to hear about what happened next with me, what happened after my diagnosis. He arrives, and we head to Starbucks.

When we get there, we see that our barista is working again, and chat with her briefly. As we were leaving from recording our last conversation, she called out to Benji. We turned to see what she wanted, and I could see that she had a slip of folded paper in her hand. He approached her, and she said it was her phone number. He took it with a smile, and we left. He told me on the car ride over here that he left her a voicemail this morning.

Normally, I would have been jealous about a cute woman giving her number to Benji, but, instead, I'm honestly happy for him. We both have been single for quite a few years, but I think he needs a girlfriend even more than I do. It is a great opportunity for him, and I'm excited about the entire situation.

We get our drinks, head toward the back, and take our places on the couch and armchair. I turn on the recorder and begin.

"Today is Friday," I say, "and we are at Starbucks getting our conversation on."

Benji begins laughing hysterically. He tries to get composed and begins. *"All right, Andrew, when I talked before, I talked about what happened after the diagnosis. Now I'm curious about your story. What were the next steps for you after being diagnosed?"*

"Okay," I say, "right after the diagnosis I entered into a period that lasted about a year and a half of trying to find the right medications for me. It was a trial-and-error process. But immediately after being diagnosed, my doctor recommended that I drop out of school. I was going to the U of M at the time, but because I had so little motivation, I couldn't do the work. I was experiencing some heavy negative symptoms from my illness. I did not want to drop out of school and move back home to live with my parents, but I had to. Every day I would wake up at 11 in the morning and go downstairs to eat breakfast. I wouldn't cook, because it was too much work to heat anything in the microwave. I'd grab something to eat cold, like a can of Spaghetti Os that I could eat straight out of the can. Next, I'd sit in a chair and rock for several hours. After sitting for so long, I would pace around the living room for a couple of hours. And, finally, I would take a shower, but only if it were shower day. I only took a shower once a week because I'd have to build up enough motivation to do it. Although I only took a shower once a week, I still had to spend several hours just to talk myself into it."

During this time at home, I wasn't interested in anything either. Previously, I had enjoyed many activities, but during this time, I had no joy whatsoever. I didn't get any enjoyment out of anything or anyone. I just wanted to be left alone. I spent much of my time during the evenings alone in my room, and I preferred it that way. I couldn't get motivated to do anything.

"I'm a little confused," Benji says. *"You say you wanted to do things, but you couldn't make yourself do them. Or you know you should have, but you still can't. How did that work?"*

"It's hard to explain. I think it is that because during these periods of psychosis, some brain damage occurs. The part of the brain that initiates activity is broken. Another reason for my lack of motivation was that things took so much effort. Often when a certain area of the brain that causes you to do an activity is broken, other areas of the brain have to take over. The other areas need to work harder to get that same task done. Consequently, simple tasks like brushing your teeth become a lot of effort. This problem is the hardest thing to explain about schizophrenia. My parents can't understand this part of my illness. And I cannot help them to understand because I do not understand it myself."

"Do you think it passes as laziness to onlookers?" Benji asks.

"Oh yeah," I say, "They don't understand how you can have this lack of motivation where you can't get anything done. For a period of time before I was diagnosed, my dad would always call me lazy and yell at me for being lazy. It was a symptom of my illness, but he didn't know that. So absolutely, a lot of times it passes for laziness."

I look around the coffee shop, assuring myself that no one is listening in on our conversation. Comforted that no one is, I continue.

"To finish my typical day, I would take a shower and have dinner with my parents. Then I would rock or pace some more, and go upstairs to my room and pace yet some more while listening to music. Finally, I would go to bed and wake up the next day just to do the same routine over again. It was boring, because I didn't really do anything—ever."

"What time would you wake up when you were having these intense negative symptoms?" Benji asks. *"Would you sleep the day*

away or did you wake up normally?"

"I would wake up late, but that is probably because of the medications. They are major tranquilizers, and very sedating. Oddly enough, I wasn't sad. From the outside looking in, you would think I was depressed. I did nothing during the day; so it looked like I was depressed. As peculiar as it sounds, I wasn't sad at all. I could be rather happy and still not get things done. It was sort of weird. At this time, I was also having a lot of hallucinations, mostly visual in nature. That threw the doctor off a little bit, because visual hallucinations are not common with schizophrenia."

"Really?" Benji asks incredulously.

"Yeah, most people think they are, but they aren't that common," I say.

When I told the doctor about my hallucinations, he wanted to make sure they were caused by my schizophrenia and not by another medical condition. Specifically, he wanted to make sure they weren't caused by epilepsy of the occipital lobe. To check whether I had epilepsy, I had to go for an electroencephalograph (EEG) test. The doctor conducts an EEG by sticking metal electrodes into your scalp, gluing them in place, and then having you look into a strobe light as you fall asleep. The electrodes detect the electrical activity in the brain, and based on that, the doctor can conclude whether you have epilepsy. The whole thing is pretty straightforward and easy, except that the night before the test you have to stay up all night long. I am used to all-nighters from my college days, but that night was incredibly hard to stay awake.

The entire day before the test you can't have any sugar or caffeine, and trying to stay awake the whole night without caffeine and while on antipsychotic medication is difficult, to say the least. My father stayed up with me, and we spent our time in the family room watching low-budget movies made in the early 1990s. After the test, the nurse tried unsuccessfully to pick all the glue off my scalp, but I was still picking glue out of my hair for about a week following the test. It turned out that I don't have epilepsy, and the hallucinations were in fact caused by schizophrenia.

"What types of things would you see when you would hallucinate?" Benji asks.

"Well," I say, "the hallucinations usually started when I was trying to drift off to sleep. The room would be pitch black, yet I would see these things of light, green or red or blue bubbles or globules of color on the ceiling that would move around and turn into geometric shapes. The shapes started to get more defined as the year progressed. One night I saw a giant eye that watched me when I was going to bed. It was sort of creepy. Then I started to have hallucinations during the day. I once saw something that looked like a snake; however, it wasn't well defined: I couldn't see scales or anything. Instead, I saw only a blue shape that sort of slithered across the parking lot."

A couple of summers ago I even saw the heavens turn red. I was out on the terrace of my parents' house, and I looked up at the sky early in the afternoon. The sky was partly cloudy, with huge, white cumulus clouds amid a bright, blue sky. The sun, which was high in the sky, turned deep red, and the sky around it turned pink, like at sunset. This experience was awesome. I felt as if I were inside the sunset looking out.

"Are your hallucinations," Benji asks, *"always things that you know are hallucinations because they are so obvious, or do you see common-day things that could blend so that you are not sure if it is a hallucination or real?"*

"Usually I can tell, like the carpet in my room will turn blue."

"Are they more surreal, more Picasso-like?"

"Usually they are. The tan carpet in my room will suddenly turn blue, so I know I am having a hallucination. Another one is seeing shadows that move. Once, I couldn't tell if what I was experiencing was real or just another hallucination. I was in my bedroom. When I closed my eyes, I saw the image of Jesus. The image was moving away from me, and I interpreted it as he was removing this veil of protection that he had around me. When I opened my eyes, I saw a demon at the end of my bed. He was looking and lurking, which really freaked me out. He was at least 6 feet tall and looked like the silhouette of a man. However, the silhouette was three dimensional and completely black. It just walked across my room looking at me. I closed my eyes and prayed. I prayed like I had never prayed before. During my prayer and while my eyes were still closed, I saw the image of Jesus return to me. When I opened my eyes, angels were hovering around my bed. The angels were sort of like the demon shape, except they were translucent white and they were hovering in midair. That was probably a hallucination, but I can't tell for sure. I went a long time thinking that one was real."

There are two reasons why I thought that experience was real. The first is because it was such a high-level hallucination. It wasn't just streaks of color, but full-fledged beings. The second is because I had seen the image of Jesus while my eyes were closed, and I don't know if you can hallucinate with closed eyes. I have always thought that a hallucination was the misperception of visual stimulation, but now I'm unsure if there needs to be a stimulus. Interestingly, deaf people can still hear voices. If that is true, then perhaps people with schizophrenia can see visions with closed eyes.

"Have you ever taken actions based on a hallucination?" Benji asks.

"Not really, not on a hallucination, because usually mine are pretty benign."

"Have you ever done anything after a hallucination?"

I don't know exactly what he means, but I try to answer. "One time it caused me a lot of anxiety. This occurred right after I was diagnosed, when I was living at home. I thought I was going to see these snakes that were about to appear on the floor and bite me, which is ridiculous, because a hallucination can't bite you. Nevertheless, I started freaking out. I would walk around the house peeking around the corner as I entered a room, because I was looking for the snakes. My parents thought I was just joking around a bit, and they started to get upset at me for making a joke of my illness. It was sort of weird."

"You talked about the visual hallucinations," Benji says, *"what about hearing voices?"*

Just as I'm about to answer, I see the barista walking toward us. She wipes off the tables as she comes over. I stop the recording, but I'm sure she overheard part of our conversation. That makes me terribly uncomfortable, because I find today's conversation incredibly personal. She leaves, and we begin again.

"Yeah," I say, "the first time before being diagnosed I did hear voices a little bit, but not too much. I couldn't tell what they were saying. After I was diagnosed and was trying to find the right meds, and while changing from one med to another med, I started hearing voices pretty much full time for like a month. Oddly enough, I heard them for so long because I didn't realize I was hearing voices. In the past they were all what are called external voices: They sound like someone is in the room talking to you. These new voices were different. They were internal voices, which sound like your internal monologue in your head, except that other people are talking and you don't have control over what is being said."

"*They are talking in your head?*" Benji asks.

"In your head. Yes, it sounds like someone is in your head talking to you. I just thought those voices were normal. I still hear them sometimes. Usually they say random things. I rarely even remember what they have said, because I don't pay attention to them. But I remember once they said, 'You better fry fish on both sides.' I was completely taken aback by it. I recall thinking, 'That was good advice,' but it was completely off the wall."

The barista interrupts us again to tell Benji that she will call him later tonight. I'm getting uncomfortable. I know that she has heard quite a bit of our conversation. I wouldn't actually mind telling her I have schizophrenia, but if she were to find out, I would need to tell her everything, paying special attention to dispelling myths about the disorder. I often think the worst myth about schizophrenia is the misconception that I will be violent. However, I'm realizing now that what is even worse is simply having someone think that I'm completely crazy. I do have meaningful and well thought-out ideas about things, and I don't like people to dismiss everything I think or say as a product of a crazy mind. I do have crazy thoughts and behaviors, but they are specific and part of a syndrome of the illness. Outside that pattern, my ideas are quite sane, and in my opinion, rather insightful.

I've always identified myself by my intelligence. Despite my IQ dropping when I developed schizophrenia, I'm usually able to hold my own with the smartest people I come across in daily life. When others find out I have schizophrenia, however, they assume I'm stupid and that my ideas are all crazy. This assumption is particularly true for my more unique thoughts. If I were sane, people would say I was "thinking outside of the box." Instead, they label me crazy, not giving my ideas any considerable thought. When they do this, in some sense anyway, it feels like they are robbing me of my identity.

The barista leaves, and we begin again.

"*She's totally messing this up for you,*" Benji says.

"Totally messing this up. So the voices in my head will say these random, demeaning things, and sometimes they make fun of me. They will even go so far as to yell insults at me. Most of the insults are usually about my weight. Thankfully, that doesn't happen too often. About half the time, the insults come from voices I don't know, and the other half of the time, they come from voices I know, usually my parents. Sometimes, I hear my brother or sister's voice. One time I heard my brother's voice say, 'Goodnight, goodnight, goodnight, goodnight,' as I was going to bed. It was pretty funny. I still hear the voices today, even though I've finally found the right meds for me. The medications aren't 100 percent effective; they aren't a cure."

"No? Are the voices less severe?"

"I can ignore them easier," I say.

"How can you ignore them now? Is it because you know through talking to your doctor, or is there something in the medicine that gives you the restraint?"

"I think it is because with the medicine, the voices aren't as loud. It is quieter in my head."

"The medication dampens it to some degree?"

"Yeah, but it doesn't erase it completely."

While I was first living at home again, I also had some paranoia, but nothing that would reach the level of fully formed delusions. Many nights I would think that assassins were coming to kill me, and so I would stay up all night long listening in the dark for them. I would only sleep if I got so tired that I passed out. I can always tell how intense my fear is by my actions. If I can lie in bed listening for assassins, then it is pretty low level. If I lie in bed listening for assassins with my clothes on, that is up one notch. If I'm lying in bed listening for assassins with my clothes and shoes on, that is up another level. If I'm fully dressed, out of my bed, and sitting in the dark in the corner of my room where I can watch the door and the windows simultaneously, that is up yet a higher level. If I am sitting in the corner but have armed myself with pepper spray, that is up at the highest level.

CHAPTER 9:
FINDING MEDICATIONS

I have felt sick all day today. I've been on a stimulant bender this weekend. Over the past two and a half days, I smoked about four packs of Marlboro Reds and drank about 27 caffeinated beverages—eight Diet Cokes, 10 vanilla lattes, and nine regular coffees. I have been going to bed about 4 in the morning the past few days, and the entire time I've felt both tired and wired.

I had two of those lattes today when I went to Starbucks with Benji to talk about our lives. We decided we were both too tired to do it, so we drove back to my parents' house, which is where we are now. We both feel like we have more energy now, so I take out my tape recorder and begin.

"It is Monday," I say, "and Benji and I are sitting in the winter garden, as my uncle Sven likes to call it, the spa room of my parents' house."

Benji breaks out laughing. "*Winter garden.*"

The spa room is a four-season porch connected to the walkout of the basement of my parents' house. It is called the spa room because there is an in-ground hot tub in the room. The rest of the room has couches and plants, and it stays warm all year round. My uncle Sven calls it the winter garden, because he is from Germany and that's the German translation for such a room. He also calls it that because he jokes that my parents and I live in a castle. Sven and his wife and three boys immigrated to the United States last August, and they have been living with me and my parents for about nine months while they save for their own housing. They are delightful people, and it is nice having them around the house.

I continue. "We went to get coffee at Starbucks, and now that I have my latte I'm fine. I also have my cigarettes, so I'm fine. So Benji, when you left the hospital, did you have the right meds? Did they figure out how to put you on the perfect combination by the time you left?"

"Well, the meds I'm on now are completely different than the ones I left the hospital on."

"How did that change come about?" I ask.

"Starting the meds in the hospital led me on the path to finding the right ones. Basically, I found in the hospital they are able to do trial and error more rapidly than they can in a clinic setting, because they can supervise 24 hours per day. So they cycled me through a few meds to see if they would have a positive or negative effect on me. I went into the hospital only taking a strong dose of lithium."

"What are you on now?" I ask.

"Now I'm on Depakote, Abilify, and I recently was put on a small dose of an antidepressant called Wellbutrin."

"How long did it take you to get on your current regimen? The regimen is working, right?"

"Yeah, excellent."

"How long did it take you to find that combination?" I ask.

"Probably two years. Two and half years."

"I'm wondering what that process was like. You went to the doctor and told him your symptoms or something? How did that all take place? They changed your meds, so how did that all work?

"Basically," Benji says, *"as I told you before, I started on the lithium, and I told the doctor that it wasn't doing anything for me. Maybe it wasn't enough lithium. Maybe if they gave me more, it would have worked. I was only on it for like a month. It wasn't long enough to tell if it was working."*

"How could you tell that it wasn't working?"

"I was still manic as hell."

"And you knew it, or did your parents tell you?"

"I was also on a bunch of tranquilizers at the time, which I forgot to mention," he says. *"I was on Trazodone, which is a tranquilizer, and I think I was on an antipsychotic medication called Zyprexa. I was also on two other tranquilizers to sedate me so I wouldn't be a harm to myself or others until I could get calmed down enough from the manic state. They were trying to bring me down, pulling me from getting worse. The idea of taking lithium is to provide a mood stabilizer. Over time, it is supposed to keep you in a stable spot, where you are not moving from mania to depression and you*

are not moving too fast. The mood stabilizers keep you from pushing the bounds, so things don't go too far down or too far up. If things go too far down, the doctors will maybe add an antidepressant, and if things go too high, they will also add an antipsychotic. Right now, I'm on an antipsychotic, a mood stabilizer, and an antidepressant, and it seems to be what works for me. But everyone's brain chemistry is different."

"That's right," I say.

"So what works for me might not be what works for the next person who walks in, and at the same time, what works for me now might not be what works for me a couple of years from now."

"Is it possible that even while on the meds you could relapse into mania?"

"It's possible, but less likely—far less likely. The chance of relapse increases when you decide not to take the meds."

"Why would anyone do that?" I ask.

"Well, there are a lot of symptoms, or side effects rather, that go along with taking the medicine. One part would just be the stigma, like if you are still in denial. The idea of not wanting a mental disorder because there is a stigma around the whole issue causes some people to stop taking their meds. The second reason that some people quit their meds is because taking lithium can make you agitated and make your hands shiver and shake."

"Like have tremors?"

"Yeah," Benji says, *"I didn't have tremors, but I was in the denial phase when I was on lithium. Other than that, lithium also has negative effects in that it can be lethal in large doses."*

"Do you have to get your blood checked?"

CHAPTER 9: FINDING MEDICATIONS

"You have to get your blood checked like every month, or every other month, to make sure it is a good level."

Benji's cell phone rings. He answers it, and it is his dad checking up on him. I think they talk at least once a day. After a few minutes, the phone call comes to an end. We continue chatting.

"So another thing I wanted to know," I say, "it seems what is particular to bipolar is that people love their mania; does that play a factor in them not wanting to take their meds?"

"At least for me, I haven't had what is called a mixed episode yet. A mixed episode means you are having depression and mania at the same time."

"So that isn't pleasant."

"If you were suicidal because of your depression," he says, *"by having a mixed episode, you are exponentially more likely to act on your impulses than just to think negative thoughts."*

"Okay."

"I haven't had such an experience as that. So part of me always yearns for that mania. It was so great—euphoria for months on end. I can't describe it. I mean coming off the high for a whole year or two years after, I continually was seeking it and wishing I could get it back."

"But you never went off your meds?" I ask.

"I never went off my meds."

"It's good."

"It is good," Benji says. *"It's kind of a coincidence. In the hospital, I had a personal nurse and she told me, 'I know that eventually you are going to get better. When you are feeling the best is when you*

*need the medicine the most.' That stuck with me and my parents.
She said it to all of us when we were there, and ever since when
I have thoughts about going off my meds, my parents remind me
of that. It lets me know that I need the meds the most when I'm
feeling good, because that means they are working. It is common
with this disorder that people start taking the medicines, and then
they feel better so they stop, because they think they don't need them
anymore—they think they are healthy. Of course, as soon as they
get off the meds, they relapse. And it's a downward cycle, because
every time you stop taking them, the chances of the same med being
as potent for you, or helping you to the same degree, gets lesser and
lesser every time."*

"You found meds that work for you," I say. "You seem very
healthy. No, you don't seem it—you are very healthy."

"I'm a walking advertisement."

"You're a walking advertisement for the pharmaceutical
companies."

"Yeah."

"Do you still have symptoms now?" I ask.

*"From time to time I get what they call hypomania, which
means I get just like modestly manic, and I get mildly depressed."*

"So you don't go to big extremes?"

"No," Benji says, *"but like for me, depression means I go to bed at
7 at night, because I have no reason to be up and just think my life is
so lame and that I have no future. I don't want to commit suicide or
anything like that. I do not even ponder it. With the hypomania, it
is just like the impulse feeling you get when you fall in love or when
you get the birthday gift you wanted. It is like a quick rush of emotion,*

kind of like the feel you get on a rollercoaster, except the rush that you feel is in your head. For example, ever since I was in my first manic state, my goal was to start my own business and have my own enterprise. Dreaming big dreams is one part of my mania. I dreamed of a venture capitalist firm at the time, but I sometimes think I can have part of my dream of being a self proprietor. I still hope it can be a dream that I can go after. So that's kind of where I now am."

"When you are having these periods of mild depression or hypomania," I ask, "can you tell, or do you only know in hindsight?"

"I know now. However, sometimes I question whether I'm really happy or if I'm hypomanic. Usually I know I'm hypomanic because the telltale signs are that I start writing in my journal immediately. Every time I get a little bit edgy or manic, I go straight to writing down all my great thoughts. I always have to write it down because I'm afraid I'm going to lose it."

"Nowadays, do you believe you have a mental illness?"

"That's an interesting question," Benji says, *"because I've never relapsed. Many people live with this disorder and go undiagnosed for years and years. I am grateful that when I got my first telltale sign of mania, I was diagnosed pretty quickly, like within probably a month or so of having the most heightened potency of mania and probably within two weeks of maybe going on just a day or two of sleep. I was diagnosed, hospitalized, and treated by all sorts of specialists around the clock to get the help I needed. In many ways I have been blessed because now I know what I have, and I know how I need to live my life. But at the same time, I know that I haven't relapsed at all, so I'm always questioning if I were to go off my meds,*

what would happen. That is the million-dollar question. Anyone in the medical profession and my family and friends would tell me that I would relapse right away. But you always wonder if it was a one-time deal, something fishy with my psyche, and I can manage it now that I know what my problem is. Can I manage it through my thought process or maybe through seeing a psychoanalyst without needing medication? I've given up a lot of things now that I take the medicine. One thing I had to quit completely was alcohol. Having to abstain from alcohol use is difficult for a lot of people, because a lot of people are codependent."

"Yeah," I say, "but it wasn't difficult for you to give up alcohol that way. You're not an alcoholic. So why was it difficult for you to give up alcohol?"

"Because, I guess, in the height of my mania, when I felt I was the shit and popular, I always went to bars and pubs. I felt at home in them. It was like Cheers, where everyone knows your name. My solution was to replace the bar with the coffee shop. However, this created another problem: The caffeine from all the coffee I was drinking was bringing on bouts of hypomania. The caffeine can increase your cycling upwards or increase the chance and the speed that you cycle upward. As a result, my doctor told me to give up the caffeine as well. For the past two months, I've been off both alcohol and caffeine, and it has been the best two months of my life."

"Wow."

"I mean," he says, "the best two months since getting diagnosed two years ago, and probably better than the three years before that, because I was having increasing symptoms then. I just didn't know it."

We take a break in our recording and Benji gets up to stretch his legs. We are ready to start again, but he remains standing and paces a bit.

"So Andrew," he says, *"you went a long time being untreated, correct?"*

"Yep."

"When did you start searching for a route of medication with prescription drugs?"

"I got on prescriptions through the first doctor I saw. I mentioned that I took the meds even though I sort of thought I was sick and sort of thought I wasn't. It's complicated, as I explained before. That is when I went on meds, and then I went to a new doctor and went on a higher dosage. Then in December 2003, I went off the meds. I did that because I didn't know what illness I had and also because I thought I was cured. I thought it was a one-time thing." Benji and I both chuckle a bit at that thought.

I continue. "I also quit the meds because I had gained 35 pounds. Sure enough, when I went off the meds, I lost 35 pounds in like two months. But then my symptoms came back, so I went to see a doctor again. And that brings me up to my current doctor, who has helped figure out the right meds for me, because now I had a diagnosis: paranoid schizophrenia. We had to see how we would treat that with medications. The first thing we tried was the med I had been placed on originally, Risperdal, because that worked well for my positive symptoms—paranoia, hallucinations, and delusions. During this time, I was having a lot of negative symptoms as well. The intense negative symptoms of apathy, loss of motivation, and lack of enjoyment lasted for a year or so. We first tried to get all the positive symptoms controlled, the hallucinations and paranoia, and we did that very well with that first med I tried. I was lucky, because usually you have to go through like seven or 10 different medications to find one that works."

I take a drink of my latte. "The one I first tried worked well on my positive symptoms, so I didn't have many of those at the time. However, the negative symptoms were pretty bad, and basically there is no med that helps with negative symptoms, except one medicine called Abilify that might help a little bit. So we decided, 'Hey, what the heck, we're going to try it,' because you just can't live life with these negative symptoms. They completely disable you. Therefore, we tried to switch over to Abilify, and as we were switching over, I was doing better."

You don't switch cold turkey from one antipsychotic to another. To switch from one med to another, you have to titrate them, meaning you slowly lower the dose of the current antipsychotic while you slowly increase the dose of the new one. The whole process takes a month or two. If you don't titrate, you will shock your system and get painful side effects or possibly become psychotic. When I had gone off my meds back in December 2003 without my doctor's knowledge, I knew enough to titrate the Risperdal down, and so I think that might be why I didn't relapse immediately.

I continue. "The second night I was on Abilify I had this sudden need to talk to people. I hadn't talked to anyone, except my parents, for like a year. And suddenly, I felt as if I woke up from a long sleep. I wanted to talk to people; I wanted to socialize; I wanted to do things. It was just amazing. I clearly wasn't back to my old self, far from it, but in comparison to how sick I had been I thought Abilify was a miracle drug. So finally we switched all the way over to Abilify, and I was no longer on risperidone, also called Risperdal."

I take a little break, and then begin again. "Then I started hearing voices, because Abilify wasn't controlling my positive symptoms, and I started getting paranoid a little bit. I saw my doctor every two weeks, and we closely monitored every symptom I had. I monitored them; my doctor monitored them; my parents monitored them. It was a collaborative effort, trying to figure out how well I was doing. Having this team with me was—and still is—important because sometimes I can't tell when I'm having symptoms, and I need someone from the outside to tell me. By carefully recording my behavior and how I felt, we noticed that I was doing the best in this period of about two weeks where I was going from one med to the other. During this transition, I was on a mix of both Abilify and Risperdal at once. Again, this doesn't work for everybody. It just happens to work for my brain chemistry. For a period of two weeks I did fabulously well, so we went back to that dosage level. That was about five years after the first onset of my symptoms. That's how I found the right meds for me. It was a lucky thing really, sort of random chance. Therefore, I have been on this same blend of medications for about three years or so now."

"*Have the side effects gone away,*" Benji asks, "*or have the posi-*

tive symptoms completely gone away now?"

"I still have side effects caused by the medication," I say. "The weight gain stays, because when I went back on the meds, I gained weight. So now I'm up 35 pounds above my normal weight, just like I was before. I'm trying to lose the weight, but it is hard. Another side effect is restless legs; it usually sets in about three to four hours after I take my meds. To counteract that, I take them at night and try to fall asleep so I don't feel the restless legs. Sometimes I get restless arms, but I do the same thing with them as I do for the restless legs. I had another side effect for about a month, not every night, but every few nights. This one is called formication, and it is the feeling of little ants or bugs crawling all over your body. It is really uncomfortable. They are crawling on your legs, arms, torso, and crotch. It is very unpleasant and hard to sleep when you feel that sensation. Thankfully, it went away. My side effects haven't been that bad though; a lot of people have them so bad that they quit their meds. To get back to your point about the positive symptoms, I still do have them every now and then."

"Do you do something different when you are having them, or do they just go away?" Benji asks.

"They go away after a while. I have a low level of trust in people; I guess you would call this a positive symptom. Basic distrust and suspicion of people is always a constant for me. Also, I will have these flair ups where I have positive symptoms. A couple of months ago, I was riding with my uncle and aunt to Red Lobster, and it was rush-hour traffic, which was causing a great deal of stress for me. Then during the dinner with my family, my brother was there with his new baby, and he was being cavalier while holding the baby. I thought it was a little bit dangerous, because I'm hypersensitive that way. My concern for the baby made me nervous. By the time I got home, I thought a serial killer was stalking me and that I was going to be tortured to death at any moment. This stressful state lasted for about three days and then went away. However, I didn't sleep at all during those three days, only when I was so tired I'd pass out. I even started carrying my pocket knife with me because I thought I would be abducted and tortured. So yes, I still have positive symptoms every now and then. I don't like surfing the Web, because I am afraid that my computer will get viruses. I am also cautious because of Internet spies. That fear doesn't go away. Yet again, I get uncomfortable when the doorbell rings and I have to answer the door, because I think it might be an assassin come to kill me; usually it is just the neighbor girl delivering Girl Scout cookies. Despite my paranoia, I still answer the door."

"When can you tell that your fears, etc., are just symptoms?"

"That's a hard question," I say. "It's called insight, and I have partial insight, which means sometimes I know they are symptoms and sometimes I don't. I didn't know the serial killer thing was a symptom. The doctor gives me these PRN meds that I can take as needed, like an extra dosage, but I didn't take them when I thought the serial killer was stalking me, because I thought it was real. Other times, I realize they are not real, but it still doesn't cause me not to be afraid. For example, if I think assassins are going to break in my room and shoot me with assault rifles, although I know it isn't real, I'm still scared, because part of me thinks it is real. It's this partial insight."

"*Are you always scared, or is it ever exciting?*" Benji asks.

"It's always scary, yet at the same time, it's exciting, because people are trying to kill me. That's pretty exciting. Being stalked beats boredom. I'd rather be scared than bored, but that is a personal preference. I think a lot of people would rather be bored. Nevertheless, the paranoia is not fun. It's never fun. It's always so scary that it freaks me out. Two days ago, I drank like five lattes and a bunch of cokes, so I was up like all night. By the time I finally went to sleep, it was 4:30 in the morning. Just as I lay down in bed, I started hearing voices. I knew one of the voices wasn't real, but it was a woman in pain, and she was moaning. It freaked me out. I knew it wasn't real, but I thought it was a spirit. It was creepy hearing this woman moaning."

"*Do you now believe you have a mental illness?*"

I break out laughing. "That's the question."

"*I mean after everything you have gone through, is it like day and night that you know?*"

"No."

"*How so?*"

"Because I don't feel crazy," I say. "I don't know if crazy has a feeling, but I don't feel it."

"*Do you feel that society has labeled you as crazy?*" Benji asks.

"No, but I just feel like me. I don't feel crazy. I realize I have crazy thoughts, but a big part of the reason I do not believe that I am crazy is that I've seen other people with schizophrenia, and they aren't as high functioning as I am. I'm pretty high functioning, so I wonder how I can have schizophrenia. I don't know if

I'm observed to be ill. I mean I have all these symptoms, tons of symptoms, and so I should know right away that I have schizo-phrenia, but some part of me . . . it's not denial either . . ." I pause to think. "Maybe it is denial."

"Have you ever thought your symptoms might get worse as you get older?"

"No, because I think I'm never going to relapse again. And thinking like that is stupid because the statistics say I will relapse; the meds just lengthen the time between relapse and reduce the number of relapses. So it is a statistical certainty that I will relapse. Despite that, I'm convinced that I'll never relapse. I'm going to get healthier and healthier and healthier the rest of my life. Furthermore, I feel like I'm over this."

"How do you deal with the statistics telling you that you are gong to relapse?" Benji asks. *"How do you think you would handle going through another long period of positive symptoms that you couldn't control?"*

"I could handle it if it were just positive symptoms. I'm plenty comfortable being scared. I'm used to that. I don't know if I could handle another period of negative symptoms, because that is when I get hopeless; the negative symptoms are bad because they prevent you from doing anything with your life. If you do relapse, it usually takes a year to two years to recover from the psychotic episode, and each period of psychosis causes physical brain damage, which I don't think you can totally recover from. I think if I had to go through that again, it would be hell. I probably could make it through, but I don't want even to think about it."

"Is that where you would have almost similar symptoms to

depression then," Benji asks, *"because of your negative symptoms?"*

"Yeah, I've been hopeless and suicidal before, but not depressed."

"Okay, so it is not that they coincide."

"I'm not sad because of a brain chemistry problem," I say. "Instead, I get hopeless because of the reality of my situation, knowing that the illness will never be cured; that is what is not too good. However, that reality is only what the statistics suggest, and I beat the statistics everyday. Every day I'm beating the statistics, and that's why I keep up hope."

CHAPTER 10:
SOME THOUGHTS II

Today has been a rather boring day. I slept late and then had a couple of hot dogs for breakfast. I managed to heat them in the microwave this time. After breakfast I showered and went to Starbucks at 50th. Benji isn't with me, but that is okay because the barista isn't working. I order my tall, vanilla, nonfat, no-foam latte and go outside for a smoke with my coffee. The man who manages the liquor store next door is outside smoking his pipe. I always love the smell of his pipe smoke, and I tell him so again today.

While smoking my cigarette, I keep thinking about how badly the mentally ill are treated. Don't get me wrong, I know that their treatment is much better today than in the past, but I still feel that I would be wiser if I hid my illness from others more often.

Benji said the first psychiatrist he saw in his rush appointment at Miami University in Ohio was nervous around him. A psychiatrist nervous around someone mentally ill? That is unbelievable to me. It is like a surgeon who can't stomach the sight of blood.

While I haven't found any psychiatrists to be afraid of me, I had an optometrist who seemed unsure how to interact with me. His strategy was to handle me with kid gloves, going the extra mile to be kind, gentle, and an all-around good guy. I remember him explaining to me that he wanted to dilate my eyes, and that he would have to put some drops in them. He then asked if that would be all right with me. I smiled and said it would be perfectly fine. It was a cordial interaction, and although I knew he was nervous, I wasn't offended by his fear of me. I understand that most people only know about mental illness from what has been portrayed in the media, and his approach of treating me nicely in the face of the unknown was refreshing.

Such cordial interactions with doctors are quite rare for me. Mostly, I'm treated as if I'm extremely stupid, even though I don't present any symptoms of cognitive impairment. Or else I'm treated like I'm not a full adult—at least not an adult with the capability to make my own medical decisions. The doctors I see for physical illnesses are often short, rough, and elitist in their interactions with me. They are the all-knowing doctors, and I'm the brain-damaged boy, simply a burden with whom they must deal so that they can afford another trip to Europe with their second wives. As a result of these sorts of interactions, I have decided not to seek treatment for anything other than my mental illness.

My psychiatrist is different though. I noticed it the first time I met him. I remember him saying, "Would that be okay with you?" It was only one line, but it was most telling of who he was. It was different than the optometrist asking my permission due to fear; in this case, asking my permission showed me that this psychiatrist actually valued me as a person with dignity. It was an affirmation that he believed my soul was still intact. He was not only going to respect that I had an opinion on my medical treatment, but he was also going to respect that I was the master of myself. He treated me as if I were fully human and part illness, as opposed to fully illness and part human.

The fear of the mentally ill is actually much worse around people who don't have doctorates. When Benji was in the hospital, not a single friend of his came to visit. Not one. I wish I had known him back then so I could have visited, but the fact that these friends—who have known him since grade school—chose not to see him due to their apparent fear illustrates the rampant stigma of mental illness.

I extinguish my cigarette and then walk to my SUV. I know the drive home is going to be nerve wracking, but I have to do it. That is a big change from who I used to be. I used to enjoy going for a drive. Early into my sophomore year at Caltech I would go on little trips during the day where I would drive to some unknown city to study in its public library. Other times, I would just go for a drive to relax. I know now in hindsight that these frequent trips were just part of the prodrome, a symptom leading up to my first episode of psychosis, but the point is that I was driving then without anxiety.

When I first became ill, many of my interests changed. And when I started losing my motivation as the negative symptoms grew, I was no longer interested in any of the activities that previously gave me enjoyment. Back when I was normal, I was interested in two different areas: athletics and academics. I loved playing sports, everything from baseball to street hockey to football. I even enjoyed sports as a spectator, mostly following football in the fall. But when my illness became severe, I no longer had any interest in sports, either playing or watching. Instead, I rocked and paced, and consequently, I was extremely bored.

The other area that interested me was academics. I loved school, but my learning didn't stop at the school doors. Starting somewhere in my junior or senior year in high school I developed an insatiable appetite for knowledge. I read regularly and prolifically. But, with the development of schizophrenia, reading no longer interested me. It was no longer pleasurable, and instead, due to the concentration it required, it was almost painful.

Today, I'm much healthier than I was five years ago. Many of my interests have come back. I'm still not playing any sports, but I am an avid football and tennis fan. My absolute favorite two weeks of the year are when the U.S. Open tennis tournament is on television; I watch almost all the coverage, from morning until night for all two weeks.

My intellectual pursuits have yet to return, primarily because I still don't have enough concentration to enjoy reading. I can force myself to read a few pages here and there if I need to, but I no longer find it enjoyable. I don't know if that will ever change.

Five years ago, I wouldn't have believed back then that I could ever become this healthy. I still have some symptoms—low intensity hallucinations and paranoia, and diminished motivation, but I don't let them interfere with my life as much as they did. The problem is that recovery is so slow that you can't ever tell if you are improving. I would often feel distressed because I feared my progress had come to a halt, when in reality I was actually getting better. I have learned that to gauge how well I'm doing, I have to compare my current level of functioning with how I was doing years ago, not weeks or even months ago. I understand that now, and so I'm not dismayed if I have a symptom or two every now and then. I know that I'm getting healthier overall, and that makes all the difference.

Chapter 11:
Disability

Benji came to pick me up today, and we drove back to Starbucks for conversation and coffee. I feel drained. It is all this talk about illnesses, I suppose. I would much rather just live my life and forget all about severe and persistent mental illness. But this illness is my life now; it isn't escapable. The tentacles of schizophrenia reach into every aspect of my life. I must come to peace with it all, and, for the most part, I think I have. I will never be who I used to be, and that sits hard in my heart. Yet again, I try to tell myself that I'm a better person for having this illness.

Nevertheless, I feel tired and unmotivated today. A coffee will help, but only so much. I pick up my tall nonfat vanilla latte, and Benji and I head toward the back. I pull out my recorder, and we begin.

"All right," I say. "Today is, I don't know, Friday, and we are . . ." A beautiful blond in her mid-20s walks by us, and I'm distracted from my thoughts as my eyes follow her movements.

"*At Starbucks*," Benji says, trying to get me to focus.

I refocus. "We are at Starbucks at 50th and France having our eighth conversation about life. So far, we have talked a bit about illnesses and have discovered that these illnesses cause disability in most cases. I was wondering, Benji, even though you have found the right medications, what disability do you find that you still have in your daily life?

"*Well*," he says, "*I don't know. I never labeled myself as having a disability, yet I have not had a steady job in two years now.*"

"Why not?"

"*I don't know quite why.*"

"Do you think it is related to your illness?"

"*Partially,*" he says, "*I mean, I was going to work in the corporate world. However, I didn't think I could handle the stress involved with those types of jobs. Subsequently, I decided to go to technical school and try to do something a little more hands on, a little more creative, and maybe with a little more liberty to work around my disability. So today I find myself one year into a two-year degree program at a technical school. I want to start my own company, because I still have that dream. I find myself not wanting to work for someone. I also still have some trouble doing manual labor. The last two summers I've started and soon quit jobs that entailed manual labor. The first job was working for a family friend doing landscape contracting. I lasted only about four weeks; I told my boss that I was too fatigued from my medicine—I just couldn't hack it. Last year I just worked at a garden retail center, and I had to wake up at 5:30 every morning to water plants. I had no motivation to get up that early. The pay was only mediocre, so that didn't motivate me either. I felt like I wasn't utilizing my skills."*

"I noticed two different aspects of how the illness was affecting your life." I say. "One aspect was the meds causing disability, which I find interesting. They seem to make you too tired and fatigued."

"I find that a lot—the meds making me too tired."

"And the other thing," I say, "is that the strategy or efforts you have to take in order to lower your stress cause you some disability."

"Yeah, there are both types. My parents don't want me to be in a position where I'm overstressed. Without their help, I would have to have a job to support myself. However, since my parents are willing to take care of me, I can take the extra steps it takes to go out there and do something healthy rather than having a higher chance at relapse."

"That sounds like it is a good strategy though."

"Yeah," Benji says, *"but it can't work for everyone, because you have to have a very supportive and financially stable family to do that."*

"How did you deal with stress when you were growing up? I mean, did you have to make similar efforts, or is this a change from who you used to be?"

"I was always the type to wait until the last minute on tests and projects and papers and stuff like that," he says. *"I did everything at the 11th hour."*

"Is that because you thrived on the stress, like having a deadline?"

"My goal was always to do the bare minimum and always get an A or B. For example, if I knew I could get As in the class, I would do the bare minimum to get the lowest A. And, if I knew it was too hard to get As because it would take too much effort, I would do the least effort to get the lowest B."

"Okay."

"And so I always found myself to be the shining star of laziness."

"How did you end up graduating," I begin, but rephrase my question. "When you graduated high school, what was your rank?"

"I was in the top 10 percent of my class."

"That's good. So you did well in school without doing much work."

"Yeah, I did well in school."

"What about athletics," I ask. "Did you play any sports or do anything like that?"

"Yeah, I did. I noticed that even in high school I got mono two times, and I still wonder to this day if part of getting mono was like going through periods of mania and wearing out my body so much that my immune system couldn't fight off the mononucleosis, or whatever it was—the virus."

"What were you doing during those periods where you wore yourself out?" I ask.

"I just found myself going on little sleep. The first time I got mono was during the ski season: I was out on the ski hill until 9 at night, four days a week."

"You were on the ski team in high school?"

"*Yeah,*" he says. "*I was on the ski hill until 9 at night, and then I was doing homework until 12 or 2 in the morning. Then, on top of all that, every weekend I would stay out as late as possible.*"

"Staying out with your friends and stuff?"

"*Yeah.*"

"You had a lot of friends?" I ask.

"*Yeah, I did. I had a great number of friends, which I was thankful for. I had a pretty gregarious social life before getting ill. Not that I have totally sacrificed that, but I feel like my social network is, you know, 1 percent or 5 percent of what it used to be. The most popular person in high school got to host the variety show at the end of the school year. I remember the person who was in charge of the student senate asked me if I wanted to host the variety show in my senior year, because the kid who had done it the past few years had graduated. I thrived on being in front of 1,000-some-odd people. I wasn't afraid of it at all at that point. And now, under the medication, being in front of 500 or 1,000 people and just talking doesn't really excite me anymore.*"

"Would it excite anybody?"

"*Well,*" he says, "*it used to excite me. I used to have dreams of getting in front of 50,000 people and giving keynote speeches.*"

Benji takes a deep long drink of his coffee and then sets it on the table. "*All right, Andrew, for yourself, do you consider yourself disabled?*"

"That is an interesting question."

"*Would you label yourself as that? I know I wouldn't label myself as that.*"

"I wouldn't," I say, "but I do have a degree of disability from this illness. Schizophrenia is actually informally called 'youth's greatest disabler,' because of the disability involved with it. For me, I'm very high functioning, so I don't have that much disability, but I do have some. I don't have a job, and I haven't had a job since I got ill. I started working for my brother once, to be his secretary, but on the second day, I had to quit because it was too much stress and was increasing my symptoms. So I do have some disability. I rarely drive in the car because of anxiety. I mean, I rarely drive myself. Sometimes, I ride with other people, but also as rarely as possible. Furthermore, I can't keep to a regular schedule every day because of lack of motivation. Usually my disability is caused by my negative symptoms, not my positive symptoms. Although sometimes even with the positive symptoms, I have some disabilities. They get in the way of friendships and relationships because there is the whole lack of trust issue. Mostly though, my disabilities stem from the negative symptoms."

Over the last few months, I have realized that my positive symptoms have been causing more of a disability than I had previously noticed. I had been having some elevated spirituality or hyperreligious episodes and because of that, I haven't been able to get my work done. It isn't that I've been distracted from work by spending all my time in prayer or anything like that. It is more from a heightened altruism. I have been trying to be an author for the past few years, and every time I get a good start on a book, I have to quit. I quit because I have been thinking that writing the books is too selfish. I am writing them to serve my own interests, instead of God's. Thus, every time I get into a book, I quit and start thinking I'm going to be an evangelist preacher instead. The hyperreligiosity is a newer problem; it started maybe a year and a half ago. Before that, my primary disability was from the lack of motivation.

After you go through a period of psychosis, you need time to heal. For me, it took two years or so. I think there are two different approaches that can be taken during this healing time. The most popular, and the one suggested by the books I have read about schizophrenia, is to view the damaged brain as a weak muscle. When you have a weak muscle, you have to train it by continuously forcing itself to do better, to lift heavier weights, or whatever. The key to that approach to recovery is to start with small tasks and force yourself (or have someone else force you) into doing more every day. The second approach is to treat the damaged brain as a broken bone. When you have a broken bone, you let the bone heal before you start using it in earnest. So you don't force yourself (or have someone else force you) to do more than you can easily do. This second approach is the one that my family and I have adopted, and I believe it could be one reason why I'm so healthy. Despite being pretty healthy, I still have a slight but persistent lack of motivation.

"Lack of motivation causes your disability." Benji says, *"Anything else?"*

"Yeah, I have the whole syndrome of negative symptoms: lack of motivation, apathy, and lack of any enjoyment. They cause me to just sort of sit around all day, and that is about all you want to do when you have them. My symptoms are not too severe, but

I do have them. Hence, all of these negative symptoms cause my disability. It is a big change from whom I used to be. I used to be this overachiever type: This geeky, nerdy, overachiever who thrived on doing well in school. I loved learning. I used to go to the library and read books; I would walk through the library and pick out books at random and read them because I just loved to learn. In elementary school, I read encyclopedias for fun."

I was actually quite advanced for my age, and I participated in gifted and talented youth programs while I was young. Interestingly, although I had started to learn the saxophone, the piano, and the trumpet in elementary school, I had little passion for music and had promptly quit playing. So I was one of the only nerds who didn't play in the marching band in high school. I did, however, take up the electric guitar in junior high for a month or two because I wanted to be a rock star. The first song I learned was *Nothing Else Matters* by Metallica, and it was the only song I had learned all the way through. I had jam sessions with a friend of mine who played the drums, but our efforts quickly fizzled out.

However, just as my intellect was advanced, so too were my fears. I remember in elementary school having many sleepless nights because of my fears that French Canadians were going to invade Minnesota, much like the Russians did to a small town in the movie *Red Dawn*.

Actually, my nighttime fears began when I was in the third grade and continued until I was a junior in high school. I never got more than a few hours of sleep a night during those years, usually passing out around three or four in the morning, only to wake up at 6 and head off to school. I even received a hand-held night vision scope one year as a Christmas gift, and many of those sleepless nights I would spend patrolling the house while it was in complete darkness. As I grew older, the fears changed from French Canadians to run-of-the-mill criminal types. These fears were only present during the night, and all day long I was free from them. Besides causing me to be perpetually tired, they didn't affect my life in any other way. I graduated from high school with a perfect 4.0 GPA, I had friends and dated girls, and I participated in extracurricular academics and athletics.

"You mentioned that you are very high functioning. Is that uncommon for your disorder, or is there a percentage of people who are very high functioning with your disorder?"

"The truth is," I say, "that I don't know. And that is because I've never met anyone who is high functioning."

"Okay."

"Not very high functioning anyway, not as high as I am. I would think that there are some out there who are, but they don't admit it. They don't come out of the closet, so to speak, and let people know. Therefore, they are all hidden somewhere, and I've never seen them. The only people I ever see are individuals who are very low functioning."

"Other than being an overachiever," Benji asks, *"what were you like?"*

"I played sports and stuff. I was pretty normal. I dated some girls. After high school, I went to Caltech. That's this prestigious science and math school, and I did well there. Well, I did well for the first year or so."

I don't have too many fond memories of Caltech, and my time there was an unhappy one. When I first went off to California, I was still dating my serious high school girlfriend, but we ended up breaking up just after the Christmas vacation. I then started drinking at the few parties that are thrown at Caltech, and I became somewhat popular among the other students.

During my freshman year, a friend of mine was an excellent guitar player, and I was hanging out in his dorm room one evening. I had his guitar on my lap and was strumming it when two beautiful women walked into his room. Caltech doesn't have many pretty women, so I think they may have been from Occidental College. They knew my friend was an excellent guitar player, and when they saw me with the guitar, they asked if I played. I put on a heavy, false macho attitude and said of course I played and that I was better than my friend. They started to get excited, and they asked me to play something. I said that I simply knew too many songs, and I couldn't possibly choose just one. Still adorning this macho attitude, I suggested that they choose a song, any song in the world, and I would play it. They turned to each other, chatted a moment, and then said to me, "Would you play *Nothing Else Matters* by Metallica?" I then proceeded to play it perfectly, guitar solo and all, and I impressed them. I still don't know if they knew that was the only song I could play.

Chapter 11: Disability

It is one of the few good memories that I have of Caltech, and I laugh thinking about it. However, since I'm far too worn out to continue, I grab the tape recorder and turn it off. We finish our coffees and head out.

CHAPTER 12:
STIGMA

It has been about two weeks since Benji and I last got together to talk about our lives. The first week he was vacationing with his parents in Naples, Fla., and I was busy looking at new cars. I haven't been able to drive much in about two or three years, and the idea in my family was that if I had a safer car, then perhaps I wouldn't be so anxious while driving. My inability to drive much has been one of the largest obstacles I have had in trying to live a more bearable life, so I agreed to give getting a new car a chance.

My father and I went to the Auto Show at the Minneapolis Convention Center, and I found two cars I liked. The first was a Volvo, which is known for its safety, and the second was an Audi. I knew that I felt comfortable in Audis because Benji drives one, and so I went to test drive both of them later in the week. Although I was leaning toward the Volvo, I found that the Audi performed better. Thus, now I'm driving a new A4. It is pretty cool, and I have already had something like four women tell me they like my car;

that response certainly seems like a step in the right direction.

Even better than the women liking my car is that I am driving again. I'm not up to the level I was at before I went on medication—I still avoid rush hour traffic—but I'm driving more and feel like I have gained a significant amount of freedom. I have even been driving in the rain, and it has been raining for the last few days pretty much nonstop.

On Sunday nights I have my mental illness support group at the church I attend. I started this volunteer ministry at my church almost a year ago, and it has been gaining traction, with more people becoming interested in it every week. The ministry has two support groups, one for people with mental illness and another one for family and friends, and we meet twice a month. I try to bring in speakers once a month too, but sometimes I fail at getting someone to come speak.

I led the support group this past Sunday and as usual, it was so stressful that it wore me out these past five days. I have been unmotivated, a little on edge, and extremely tired all week. I don't like that my group meeting does this to me. I become basically incapacitated for a week afterwards, but it is so important to everyone who attends that I don't feel I can abandon it.

My mental health was good up until Sunday. I was in such good spirits because of my new car that earlier in the day on Sunday I asked a woman at a coffee shop for her phone number. She is a nice, sweet, pretty woman, and I was very happy to see her whip out a pen, grab some paper, and jot it down for me. I called her on Tuesday, but I got her voicemail. It has been several days now, and I still haven't heard back from her. My impression is that I won't ever hear from her. That is a little disappointing, and I wonder if it has added to my unproductive week so far.

Today I feel better though, so I invited Benji over to my parent's house to talk about our lives. When he arrived, I grabbed him a caffeine-free Diet Coke and grabbed myself a Diet Cherry Coke, and we headed downstairs to the spa room.

I immediately notice that Benji is flying high because of his new love with the friendly barista and is in an incredibly playful mood. I pull out a pack of Marlboro Reds and light a smoke. He takes the pack from me and lights a cigarette for himself. He is a nonsmoker, and I remember one night we were walking around the Uptown neighborhood in Minneapolis when he bummed a cigarette from me. He took about three puffs and then started coughing and ended up puking on the sidewalk. I tell him not to puke in the house, and he assures me he won't. I set my recorder on the table, and we begin.

I say, "Today is Friday..."

"*Friday,*" Benji blurts out simultaneously.

"Thanks, Benji," I now wonder if he is in too good a mood today. "We are sitting in the winter garden . . ."

"*As Sven calls it.*"

"As Sven calls it, instead of at Starbucks because it is raining, and we didn't feel like going to Starbucks."

"*I didn't want to bombard my lady friend, in case she is working.*"

"We didn't want to bombard her either," I say, "because you see her too much."

"I just didn't want to make it awkward for her coworkers."

"Okay. Today I was thinking of talking a little bit about stigma. What is stigma, Benji? Do you know?"

"No, I don't," he says playfully, apparently still on his high from his new love. *"Would you explain it?"*

"The textbook or rather the dictionary definition would be 'the branding of shame or a mark of disgrace.'"

"Like smokers have?" Benji says as he blows out a huge puff of smoke into the air.

"Like smokers have, I suppose," I say. "Stigma seems to be this general prejudice that normal people have against people with mental illness. They fear that people with mental illness will be violent, or they may think that people with mental illness deserve their illness because they are weak willed or have weak morals."

The common line for advocates of the mentally ill to say is that the mentally ill are not any more dangerous than the average person. While that is true of most mental disorders, it isn't quite true for schizophrenia. There is a slight, elevated risk of violence from people with schizophrenia, and it is almost always from people with schizophrenia who are both unmedicated and are abusing drugs and/or alcohol.

Over the years, Hollywood and the news media have vastly over-exaggerated the dangerousness of the mentally ill to make greater profits, and much of the blame for stigma should fall squarely in their laps. Today, they both are doing much better at restraining themselves from sensationalizing tragedies involving the mentally ill, but in one respect I think they continue to fail.

A preoccupation persists in these circles to explain human action completely in terms of psychology. Today, murderers and criminals and the like are no longer called evil; they are called disordered. Every unthinkable act of evil is then attributed to a mental illness. Murderers become psychotic, and child molesters become sick. The truth is that for someone to have a mental disorder, for someone to be crazy, they must have a specific pattern of thoughts and behaviors. Not every weirdo and pervert is mentally ill. You have to be weird in a certain way that can be attributed to having a specific chemical imbalance in the brain.

In the rare case that a person with schizophrenia is violent, that violence is often moral within his or her psychotic reality. For instance, a psychotic man might lash out at a police officer who has cornered him, and that would be an immoral thing to do in objective reality. However, in the reality of the psychotic person, it may very well be moral because in his or her reality, the police officer is there to kill the man. The person must accordingly act in self defense.

What I have found in myself is that when I have had serious paranoia about people trying to kill me, I have simply isolated myself and retreated to a safe place. I never feel like lashing out, and I imagine that this pattern is also true of others with schizophrenia. One strategy that I have employed in dealing with paranoid thoughts comes from my strong religious faith. I make a conscious effort to forgive the people who are plotting against me. I don't actually go up to the people and say that I forgive them. Instead, I forgive them in my heart for perpetrating such evil against me. It isn't an easy thing to do, but once you completely forgive someone for doing these horrible things against you, there is no reason for arguments or hateful thoughts. This strategy is what has kept my interactions with family and friends cordial.

Benji starts laughing loudly. I don't think I have said anything funny, but then I figure out why he is laughing, and I give out a chuckle. When he tried to ash his cigarette, the lighted end completely fell off his cigarette and into the ash tray.

"We are having a good time today," I say, "even though it is sort of rainy out. We haven't recorded in a while, haven't had any of our conversations."

"Because you have been sick."

"I've been a little bit troubled by my illness. But today we are coming back to our conversations, because I think I'm healthy enough to get back to work. Thus, I was saying that stigma is when people think the mentally ill are weak willed or that they have weak morals, it suggests that the mentally ill deserve their fate or that they are sinful or something like that. Those stigmas are very common. Thankfully, it is getting better, I think; I've heard that they were really bad a long time ago."

"Yeah, it was bad back in the '60s," Benji says.

"And there is still quite a bit of stigma associated with bipolar and schizophrenia, as opposed to depression. I know a woman at church with depression. Another woman told her that her walk with the Lord must not be right because of the depression. She actually had manic depression. There is stigma associated with depression too. How do you decide when you are going to tell someone you have a bipolar disorder?"

"*Well,*" Benji says, "*you have to decide whether you are going to let someone into your inner circle.*"

"Okay."

"*Your inner circle of trust is what I like to say,*" he says playfully. "*The trust circle.*"

"I know that movie."

"*As Robert De Niro would say.*"

"You're very much like Robert De Niro, aren't you?"

"*I'm cool like him,*" Benji says flatly, but obviously being playful.

"So you've decided to let someone into your inner circle of trust. How do you decide that?"

"*Well,*" he says, "*you have to know them for a little bit. Or you just have to know. It is almost like risking it all, because as soon as you tell you can't take it back.*"

"Right, you can't unring that bell."

"*Good quote,*" Benji says as he starts chuckling. "*Basically, I have been told to never ever, ever tell.*"

"Why is that?"

"*Unless it is family or close friends.*"

"And why are you not supposed to tell?" I ask.

"*Well, with employers it causes havoc; you might not get a job you are interviewing for.*"

"Have you seen any of that?"

"*I'm having trouble right now finding a job, because I have a two-year void on my résumé,*" he says.

"Yeah. So they look at the void and what do they say?"

"*They ask, 'What did you do for those two years?' I answer, 'I had some health issues, and I couldn't work.' And they know they can't ask, and I don't tell.*"

"But they know . . ."

"*I had an interview yesterday, and I got asked that exact same question.*"

"Okay," I say.

"*'What did you do for those two years, Ben?' And I was like, 'I had a health issue that prevented me from working.'*"

"So they can decide not to hire you because of that—if you don't answer it satisfactorily?" I ask. "They can say they aren't going to hire you for whatever reason, and it is really because they know you have a health issue."

"*Yeah,*" Benji says. "*It is supposed to be disguised so it can't hurt you, but having a void on your résumé always hurts you.*"

"That is one thing I was afraid of when I was getting healthier and thinking about getting a regular job. I have all these years of unemployment and doing nothing. Of course, the first thing they would ask would be what did you do, and I couldn't answer that to their satisfaction. I could lie, but if they found out I lied in the interview, they could fire me. It seems like it is a no-win position. Do you feel that way?"

"*Yeah.*"

He pulls out another cigarette from my pack and lights it. I'm surprised and ask him, "Are you going to chain smoke today or what?"

"*Yeah. I'm feeling like it. This is the day I become a smoker.*"

"You shouldn't become a smoker. It is bad news."

There is a pause in our conversation, but then he continues. "*In general, you shouldn't tell.*"

"Because of the stigma?"

"*Because of the stigma. It is also hard when you meet people. If you want to date someone, they'll ask, 'What do you do.' And for you or me, it is like, well, I've been unemployed for two years. You, longer. You're always like, 'I'm an author.' And they're like, 'Sure, whatever.'*"

"Yeah, they don't believe me," I say.

"*With me, I'm in school again, and I tell them I go to school, and they ask, 'Do you work?' I say, 'No, because it will be too much stress on me and will pull me back into mania possibly.' Nevertheless, I have to get a job for the summer, and I'm hoping it won't wear me out. I have this problem with physical fatigue. I'm hoping that if I get a manual labor job this summer, I can make it through.*"

"For me," I say, "I've always heard 'never tell,' just like you. Despite this advice, I've done something different. At one time, I thought there would be no way that I would ever get healthy enough where it mattered if I told or not, and so I decided to tell everyone basically. I have become open about my illness."

"*How's that working out for you?*"

"I don't know. I don't have a girlfriend yet. I try not to tell women."

"*What happens when you tell them?*" Benji asks.

"Basically they get scared off. I was on e-Harmony, the online dating site, and I had conversations with a couple of women. It was going along well, and then I told them that I had a mental illness that was treated properly and that I had no symptoms. One of the women, who is a mother with young children, was scared. She told me she thought I might hurt her children—even murder her children—so, she couldn't date me. Even though she was interested and we had a good rapport, learning about my illness scared her away. That is generally what happens."

"*Have you gotten hurt in the past other than that?*" Benji asks.

"Yeah, sort of. I don't want to get into it though. I know what you're alluding to, but I don't want to talk about it. It is just too painful of a memory."

"*Fine.*"

"Generally that is the case. You can't get women to date you. When looking for work, if the employer knows you have schizophrenia, there is no way they would hire you."

"*I tell people more than I should.*"

"You told the barista," I say.

"*Yeah, I did tell her. Well, you were writing this book while we were at Starbucks, and she was intrigued by the book, and we would allude to what it was about, but we never said it was about mental illness. We said it was about this, about that, about overcoming struggles. And she said, 'Wow, that is interesting,' and I told her, 'If you go out with me, I will tell you what it is about.' She agreed, and, in an hour and a half, I told her my whole life story about mental illness.*"

"How did she take it?"

"*She liked it,*" Benji says. "*She said she wishes she were more interesting.*'"

"She wishes she was more interesting?"

"Yeah. I said that everyone has one person in the family who is screwed up. And she said, 'Nah, I don't have that in my family; no one is screwed up.'"

"That's funny. And she has gone out with you several times."

"Yeah, it is working out so far."

"That's great," I say. "It is very unusual though."

"Very unusual. I'm happy now. I'm in a good place right now. What's on my face right now?"

"A smile. A huge smile."

"A grin."

"A grin." I take a sip of my Coke. "I met a woman at a coffee shop last week, and she gave me her number. I called her once, but she hasn't returned my call. And I'm trying to debate how and when I should tell her I have schizophrenia. I have been doing a lot of speeches around the city, and so I'm sort of well known in certain circles, so it is harder to hide it. Therefore, I'm thinking the best thing to do is to come right out and tell her I have schizophrenia, but that I'm high functioning and don't have that many symptoms. Well, I'll say I don't have any symptoms."

"You're like John Nash," Benji says.

"I'm like John Nash? Not quite. I'm not as smart and not as symptomatic. I'm trying to figure out how to tell her if she ever returns my phone call, so that is what has been weighing on my mind. Part of what worries me is that she might already know because many people at the coffee shop know that I have schizophrenia, so a worker might have told her and that is why she isn't returning my call. So I always have a worry in the back of my mind about who knows and who doesn't know, and it doesn't matter too much if I tell them because I know that they will either accept it or not right away. Still, I'd rather tell someone personally than have them find out second hand."

"*Like secondhand smoke; it really kills,*" Benji says as he exhales a cloud of smoke.

"Like the secondhand smoke that you are blowing in my face."

I turn off the tape recorder, and we slowly finish our Cokes.

CHAPTER 13:
SOME THOUGHTS III

I'm getting healthier. But now I have a new added stress—the stress of getting healthy. It seemed odd to me at first, but I have felt it increasing for a year now, and I'm fearful that it will make me relapse. The stress of getting healthy could also be called the stress of expectations, because that is what causes it.

Most of the stress I'm experiencing is caused by my parents. My mental illness is largely an unseen one, especially as I become healthier, and so my parents assume I'm healthier than I am. So they raise the bar of expectations of what I should be able to accomplish, and they desire that I meet this new level. In reality, I'm not healthy enough to meet this new bar, and trying and failing to meet it causes enough stress to increase my symptoms and possibly send me into a relapse of psychosis.

But as I do get healthier, the bar of expectations must rise, because I'm doing more and engaging in more activities. The difference is that I'm the only one who can be in a position to know where the bar should be set. I don't have a job. People often look at me and wonder why, because I look so healthy. In truth, I am this healthy because I don't have a job, and adding a job on top of everything would pull me back into psychosis. If I manage my stress and keep it low, I can keep healthy.

It often feels that there is never a time when I can actually enjoy life. This is because of the expectations. The bar rises faster than I can keep up, so I never have a chance to say I'm doing well, because I always fall short of the bar. That is particularly true when I'm in a good mood but still have persistent negative symptoms. If I look like I'm in a good mood, people assume that I'm fine. But I'm not fine; I'm pretty far from fine. That only real time I can relax is when I'm in a terrible mood or even suicidal, because then everyone lowers their expectations. I often feel like I need the world to stop for a minute so I can take a breather, because battling this illness is so emotionally and physically draining. If I'm ever in a good mood, I can't just take a breather, because up go the expectations.

Still, in all honesty, I can't only blame others for all of this stress; some of it I put on myself to achieve. For instance, I put a lot of pressure on myself to have a career. I don't want to feel like a parasite on my parents; that is how I feel much of the time. So I put a lot of pressure to get a career, but so far all the efforts have fizzled out. I have even tried to go back to college a number of times, but nothing seems to work.

In the meantime, I have tried to do volunteer work to ease me back into a position where I can do actual paid work. Most of these efforts are expended through the Barbara Schneider Foundation.

I first learned of the foundation through a friend of a friend of my mother's. She has a brother with paranoid schizophrenia and serves on the board of directors of two nonprofit organizations in Minneapolis. The first is called Tasks Unlimited and is a lodge program of supported housing and employment. The second is the Barbara Schneider Foundation, which is an advocacy group that promotes better law enforcement response to mental illness through a program of specialized officers trained in a model called Crisis Intervention Teams (CIT).

When I heard law enforcement mentioned, my ears perked up. Back when I was in high school I participated in a police explorers program and was considering going into law enforcement after college. Then she asked if I wanted to come to a board meeting and check it out.

That meeting started my involvement with the foundation, and later I was made a member of the board and, soon after, policy chair of the organization. Helping this organization has shown me that under the right circumstances, my illness can be viewed as an asset, not a liability. I can't say I have helped enormously, but I hope I have made some impact by my presence. In addition to serving on the board, I give talks to the officers undergoing the specialized CIT training. In the talks I basically go through my experience with mental illness and answer any questions that may arise from my speech. Besides pure education, I'm also trying to put a face on mental illness for the officers. So far it seems to be working well, and the officer trainings have been a smashing success.

CHAPTER 14:
FAMILY RELATIONSHIPS

I have been dreading the thought of today's conversation. About a month ago, I got the idea that Benji and I should sometime talk about our families, and ever since then I have been apprehensive. I know that the impact of our illnesses on our families needs to be discussed, but I also know what needs to be said will probably hurt people we love. Not that anything I have to say is mean spirited, but much of my thoughts about my family are products of a deluded mind.

When I asked Benji to join me for another of our conversations, I requested that we discuss matters in the spa room of my parents' house. Having this conversation might cause me to get teary-eyed, or in the very least too emotional to discuss in public at Starbucks.

Benji has just arrived, and as I grab him a caffeine-free Diet Coke, we head toward the spa room. My recorder is in hand, and my Diet Cherry Coke is waiting for me on the coffee table. We both take a seat, with me in a rocking chair and Benji on the couch.

"Today," I say, "is Tuesday. We are sitting in the winter garden again talking about our lives, the 10th of our recorded conversations. Today, I thought we would talk about how our illnesses have affected our family. So Benji, do you have brothers and sisters? What does your family do and things like that?"

"*I have one sister,*" Benji says, "*who is three years younger than I am. My family is pretty much the American dream of a family.*"

"Okay, so your parents are still together?"

"*Still together after 25 years. My dad works; my mom kind of works—just not to make a living.*"

"Just for fun?" I ask.

"*Just for fun.*"

"When you were younger, did she work, or was she a housewife?"

"*She worked as a teacher for a while, but lately she hasn't worked much.*"

"What about your sister? Does she work or is she in school?"

"*She is a junior in college,*" Benji says.

"What does she study?"

"*Accounting.*"

"Oh, like your dad."

"*Yes. Accounting is something I could never study, because I feel the need to be creative.*"

"How did your family find out that you had a mental illness?" I ask.

"*They found out when they got a phone call from the mental health office from my university.*"

"How did they take it? Do you know?"

"*They panicked.*"

"They panicked?"

"*As soon as they received the phone call, they boarded a private jet. Within four hours, they were there to take me away.*"

"At that time did they believe you had a mental illness?" I ask.

"*They didn't know.*"

"Okay," I say, "so later on when they did know, were they in denial or did they accept it?"

"*I think my mom was in denial a little bit; my dad was pragmatic, so he pretty much went with whatever the doctors were telling him. Basically, he was willing to do whatever it took to support me.*"

"Is your mom still in denial?"

"*I wouldn't say she is, but I think sometimes she is in denial of my capabilities. I think I have lower expectations for myself than before my illness, and sometimes she doesn't like that I adhere to those lower expectations.*"

"Is it hard on you that she still has those high expectations for you?"

"*No, not really,*" Benji says. "*I know she loves me either way. It's just that she feels a little guilty, as if she did something wrong as a parent, which she didn't. Or she wonders if there were signs ahead of time she could have witnessed so I could have gotten help earlier instead of having to go through psychosis, have an actual family crisis, and be hospitalized. She was a school counselor for a long time, and she thought she was pretty familiar with problems, adolescent problems. However, I was a pretty normal kid growing up. So my illness took her completely by surprise.*"

"Did you have mental illness in the family before you got sick?" I ask.

"*No. We had alcoholism, but every family seems to have that.*"

"So you are the lucky one."

"*Right.*"

"The genetic lottery," I say, but Benji doesn't find it very funny. I move on. "How does your family support you?"

"*Well,*" he says, "*they support me completely financially—pay my rent, pay for my car, pay for my gas, and pay for all of my food. I've had a lot of difficulty finding any employment. I found a part-time job this winter teaching ski lessons. Besides that, I haven't found any steady employment the last two years.*"

"Do they support you emotionally at all?"

"*Yeah.*"

"They live out of state, right?" I ask.

"*They live out of state now, but I talk to them every day. So they support me emotionally.*"

"What do they do, or what could they do to help you more? Could they do anything?"

"*I don't think so.*"

"They do everything possible?"

"*A lot of things you have to figure out on your own. I think some people like to help other people, but I also think people with different disorders have to learn to live with them on their own.*"

"To clarify, you mean the people who suffer from the illness need to learn to live with it independently?"

"*Yeah,*" Benji says, "*I mean, my family can help me financially, and they can help me modestly with support and encouragement,*" *but at the end of the day, I have to learn how to live with my situation. They can't do that for me—there is no magic pill they can give me. I take magic pills that I get from the doctor, and they seem to help a lot. The most important thing my family can do is help to make sure I have a steady influx of the medication that makes a difference. This medication is my life support right now. Without it, I could dip back into some serious, serious hole, and maybe not be able to dig my way out. So the possibility of not affording the meds is a big worry, because, in another six months, I will lose my insurance through my family. I'll have to find a way to get insurance on my own, or else my parents will have to opt to buy me individual insurance, which is what probably will have to happen."*

"Is there anything they do that you wish they didn't do?" I ask. "Anything that doesn't help?"

"Well," he says, *"for a while they were constantly asking me what they could do. They were sending me to a psychologist twice a week, which I enjoyed thoroughly. A lot of people like therapy, but a lot of people don't like it as well. Honestly, I don't know if I got anything out of it; all I know is that I enjoyed it. It was something to do that kept me from being bored. When my parents initially panicked, they did things like taking away my car. I didn't drive for a month, because I was just a little psychotic. Therefore, I had to gain back their trust to drive the car again, and I had to always let them know where I was going and things like that."*

Benji takes a drink of his Coke and then continues. *"But for months and months after my initial manic episode, I was always trying to regain that mental high, because I was in denial myself. And even if I knew I had something, I would rather live with it than try to cope with it. I would go on these little journeys around town trying to find ways to continue on my manic quest, which were basically these little idiotic dreams I tried to fulfill: like becoming an actor or being an entrepreneur and starting my own enterprise. I'd go to coffee shops and meet strangers."*

He gets up to pace a bit. *"I remember meeting this old man; I think he also had some sort of mental disorder. He had a bicycle with a patent on it. He didn't actually have the patent, but on the bike it said 'patent pending.' It was a bike that you would pump like a stair climber instead of cycle, and he had been trying to sell his patent for about 15 years. He just peddles around town hoping someone with money will see his bike and buy it from him. I flagged him down one day. I tailgated him and flashed my lights at him until he pulled over, and I asked to have coffee with him. I did all this because I thought I could help him reach his dream, and vice versa. Another day I met the CEO of the Timberwolves, and I was convinced he could give me a job. I had his card and I was just about to call his secretary to set up a meeting with him to talk about employment, but luckily my dad stopped me before I called. I've done things like starting to write letters to different CEOs all over the world and famous people whom I want tell about my ideas. I was constantly realizing that I didn't know where to mail the letters, or if I did know, I realized that the letters would never get to them, because they would get filtered. But when you are in the manic period, everything seems possible. So you continue to try."*

"How have your relationships with your family members changed because of your illness?" I ask.

"They've gotten stronger. It used to be that you only share with

your parents what you want to share, but after I was sent to the hospital, the doctors pretty much interrogated me like I was a criminal. Since my parents were there, I had to tell them everything I had ever done, like experiment with drugs or abuse alcohol. My parents just sat there and listened to it, whether they wanted to or not. Now it is like, if anything happens, I might as well just tell them, because what does it matter? They already know all of the other bad stuff. As a result, our trust is a lot stronger; I know that no matter what, they are going to support me. Even with all their help, I'm trying to live my own life now, but I'm constantly reminded that employment is difficult to find. I even have a college degree from Miami of Ohio, but there's that huge void of not doing anything for two years. It's hard to convince employers why I'm employable when I have just been a vagabond for two years."

"What does your family say about that?" I ask.

"*I don't know.*"

"That you might not be able to get a job this summer."

"*I don't know. We'll see.*"

"Do they put pressure on you to get a job?"

"*No, this time the pressure is all self imposed. Last summer I got pressured to have a real job, like a profession, and I had a lot of difficulty for the same reasons. Understandably, it is hard for anyone to get a job out of college. Yet, it wasn't just that. My dad put a lot of pressure on me then to get a job, and it didn't work out.*"

I can tell he doesn't feel like saying too much more, so I turn off the recorder. We take a break for a few minutes, and I have a smoke. I know that it will be my turn next to talk, and I'm dreading it. Benji still hasn't sat down from his pacing, and I wonder if this is a hard topic for him too. Five to 10 minutes pass, and I turn the tape recorder back on.

"Andrew," he says, *"what is your family like?"*

"My parents are still together. They just had their 30th anniversary. My dad is retired. He was an entrepreneur and electrical engineer. My mother is a housewife and has been ever since I was little. I have an older brother who is three years older, and he is a lawyer who owns his own practice. I have a younger sister who is married and is a mother and housewife; I think she is also a cosmetologist on the side. It is a pretty typical family."

"How long ago did they find out about your mental illness?"

"I don't know when my brother and sister found out about it," I say, "but I remember telling my parents that I thought I was ill before I got diagnosed or before I was in treatment. That was early summer of 2003. I had researched it on the Internet and went out and bought a book called *Diagnosis Schizophrenia*. This book is written for people who have just been diagnosed. It is a real easy read for people who have trouble reading and concentrating. I read it and thought, 'Yep, that's me.' My parents wanted to know what was going on with me, what was wrong with me. So one night I gave them the book and said that they had to read the whole thing through before I would talk to them. My dad read the book, but, well, my mom didn't. She said she did. However, when I pressed her with some questions, she said she didn't, but that my dad had told her all about it. Then I told them I had schizophrenia, and my dad said, 'No, you don't,' and he didn't buy it. So that is how they found out originally."

"*Interesting.*"

"Then I went into treatment for an unknown mental health condition. I thought I had schizophrenia, my mom thought I had schizophrenia, but my dad did not. I think it was a little hard on him accepting that I was ill, because I was his son, and I was so normal growing up. I think he thought of mental illness like mental retardation, like you have it your whole life. He didn't see me as mentally ill, so he didn't accept it for a long time. I mentioned earlier that he would get mad at me for being lazy, and this was before I was diagnosed, but he wouldn't accept that I had disabilities or these symptoms. He would, instead, think it was me personally, as opposed to my illness that was causing it. So instead of thinking that I had a lack of motivation because of my illness, he would think I was lazy because of my character. I understand his denial, because it is easier psychologically to think you have a son who is a little bit lazy than to think he has a serious illness. It is hard to accept that your child has one of the most serious illnesses known to man."

I take a sip of my Coke. "That is how they found out. I don't know how my brother and sister found out. I must have told them, or my parents must have told them. I remember telling my extended family, and I was nervous because I didn't know how they would react. They were talking about the movie *A Beautiful Mind* at a family reunion and saying that the movie was so good and that kind of thing. Soon after, I went out with my uncles to a bar. We were drinking heavily, and that is when I told them I have schizophrenia. They said, 'Oh, okay.' They didn't really care. The funny thing is that I've gotten a very good reaction from my extended relatives. Since word of mouth traveled fast, they all quickly found out that I was ill. They said, 'If you're on meds, you're fine.' I don't correct them, because they think the meds are a cure or something. They don't understand how severe the illness is, but that's fine. I don't really care if they think I'm healthier than I am. They've all been great. Everyone has been pretty good to me."

"*What does your family do to support you now?*" Benji asks. "*What do they do that sustains you?*"

"Okay, well, similar to you, everything financially. I'm living at home and pay no rent. Soon I will be moving into a new condo that they paid for. They pay for my health care, my medicine, and my food. My mother has been doing my laundry, but I'm doing more of that now. I'm taking over more things as I get healthier."

"*Do you find,*" Benji asks, "*that you need less support as you're learning to live with your illness, or does it depend on the day?*"

"It depends on the day," I say. "But I'm not learning to deal with the symptoms. I can't learn to deal with the lack of motivation, how to overcome it. However, as I get healthier, it is less of an issue. So as I'm getting healthier, I'm taking over more tasks. But on the days when I'm not healthy, things don't get done. My family supports me by taking over the things I can't do: Cleaning my clothes, doing the dishes. I don't help out around the house at all. Actually, I don't do much at all. They take care of every need I have, and that frees me up to do more meaningful things. In turn, I am better able to cope with my illness, I suppose, because it allows me to live a life I consider worth living. Having a worth-

CHAPTER 14: FAMILY RELATIONSHIPS

while life is important because I didn't have one not so long ago. Emotionally, they don't help me at all, because I don't let them. I am very independent. Even though I'm completely dependent on them, I'm an independent person. I don't rely on anybody for emotional support. I do it myself. I went to see a therapist a couple of years ago for a few sessions, and I didn't get anything out of it. I was just managing to support myself."

"You said you are independent and don't rely on your family for emotional support. Has that changed since your illness, or were you always like that? Also, has your relationship with your family members changed due to your illness?"

"No," I say, "well, my relationship with my family has changed, but with the emotional support factor, I have always been independent. I was so independent that they used to call me the 'Lone Wolf.'"

"Do you think you should be more dependent now, because you will need support at times?"

"I am more dependent," I say, "just not emotionally. And that isn't a change. Nevertheless, my relationship with my family has changed quite a bit because of my illness. Basically, it has brought the family closer together. I wasn't that close to my family while I was growing up. Now, I am much closer to each of them. I talk to my brother quite often, and I talk with my sister quite frequently also. And I'm closer with my parents. When I was growing up, my dad was pretty much always working. However, now that he is retired and I'm living at home, I have an opportunity to talk and hang out with him more. We have a closer relationship now, and I have gotten to know him better as a person. That is certainly a positive change."

I light a cigarette before continuing, hoping to set my nerves at ease. "There have been some negative changes in my family relations because of my illness. Although my relationship with my brother is closer and stronger, there was one time when I thought he was plotting to take over a business I was starting. Obviously, that strained the relationship for a few days, but that paranoia is gone. I have had other negative thoughts about the people that I love, so that is hurtful to me and hard for me to handle."

The business I'm referring to is called Risen Man Publishing, and it is my desperate grasp at living a productive life. I am hoping to publish all the books I write through this company, and I hope that I will be able to grow it and publish the works of others, too. I don't know if I will ever be healthy enough to run it. My father is helping me out with the venture, and my dream is that by the time the business is actually printing books, I will be healthy enough to take it over from my father.

My brother incorporated the business for us, and it was during this time that I thought he started his plot to take it over from me. The business right now is in name only, but my fear was that my brother would lie in wait until we were a huge empire and then try to take it by having the courts rule me incompetent or by getting me committed. I can see now that he is not the type to do this, but at the time it seemed not only possible but probable.

I continue. "With my sister, I haven't had any paranoia."

I don't know why exactly I have paranoid thoughts about some people and not about others, but with my sister I have never had any such thoughts. Part of the reason may be that she lives out of state, so I have minimal contact with her, apart from phone calls.

"With my mother," I say, "I was always very distrustful of her. It is not that I fear she is a spy or a secret agent, but I've suspected that she snoops on me all the time. I don't know if she does or not, but I always have thoughts that she does. This paranoia made it hard to have a relationship with her for a long time—a real relationship other than just saying hello and goodbye and things like that. We have come to a relative peace now, because she isn't allowed in my room. She hasn't been in my room and I haven't invited her into my room for something like two years. She is not allowed up there because I think she would snoop through all my stuff. I don't know if that is paranoia—it probably is—but that hurts my relationship with her. There was another time where I had just seen a movie called *Momento*, about a guy who is losing his memory and as a result, he has to tattoo on himself everything he wants to remember. There was a point when I thought, after seeing the movie for the third time, that if I were going to lose my memory and had to tattoo one thing on my body to remember, it would be, 'Don't trust mom.' This thought makes me sad. So that was tough."

I take a deep drag off my cigarette. "As for my dad, people with schizophrenia are often hypersensitive to criticism and stressful environments, and my dad's criticism caused me lots of stress. Not so much anymore, but about three years ago, it did. It was either just before or after I was diagnosed, and I was quite suicidal. He was causing me lots of stress, which would increase my suicidal thoughts. Consequently, I started to believe that he was intentionally causing me stress because he was trying to get me to kill myself. I believed that for about a year. Obviously, these hurtful thoughts caused a strain on my relationship with him. Even one weekend when my parents went away on vacation and left me home alone, I spent most of the time hiding in my room because I thought my father had hired a hit man to kill me. That delusion also hurt my relationship with my dad. Thankfully, those thoughts are all past now. We have grown a lot closer and are having a lot better time. Overall though, I feel that my paranoia has damaged relationships."

I don't know why I thought that my father had hired a hit man to kill me, but at the time it just seemed like something he would do. Similar to my paranoid thoughts about my brother, this paranoia is so ridiculous that it would make you laugh, provided that it didn't have such negative repercussions on my family relationships. It was a long time ago now, so I suppose it doesn't matter. I turn off the recorder, finish my cigarette, and light another one.

CHAPTER 15:
FRIENDSHIPS

———————

Although it is April, we are having a cold spell in the Twin Cities. It must not be any warmer than 20 degrees. Most of Edina is away in warm places. It is spring break for Edina public schools, after all. I was supposed to go to Palm Springs with my family, but I opted out at the last minute. Vacations are usually too stressful for me, and by the time I return home, I need another week or so to relax. I can't afford such a setback right now. Anyway, my life is such that I don't need a vacation away from anything. I don't have a job that I need to get away from, and I like the consistency of my life. I suppose it is too boring, but more excitement than what I'm used to might set me back. I dread the thought of having to go through a period of long recovery should I relapse into psychosis.

I'm outside right now smoking a cigarette with one of the waiters here at Perkins. Perkins is a chain of family diners that is open 24 hours a day, and it is one of my favorite places to go later in the evening. The coffee is cheap, and, for less than $2, you can have a bottomless cup. They always have ridiculous music playing, and that adds to the special ambiance of the place.

The waiter I'm outside with has served me and Benji before, and I'm a little disappointed that I don't know his name. One evening he even gave us free coffee and muffins. We talk about the weather, and then he goes inside. When Benji arrives, we go in and ask for a remote table. Even though only a few people are in the restaurant, we get seated in the far room, the place formerly designated for smoking. The waiter I had just been smoking with approaches, and I order a carafe of regular coffee. Benji decides on a carafe of decaf and a club sandwich. The waiter leaves, and I take out my recorder. Before we begin, Benji shows me the portfolio he is compiling. It is full of landscape designs that look professional. He is very excited about his portfolio, and I am impressed with his work. I hope he will soon get a job where he can use his skills. The job hunt hasn't been easy for him, and it seems that everywhere he turns, he hears a resounding no. I think he will have more success in the interviews with his new portfolio, and I tell him so.

After half a cup of coffee, I turn on the recorder, and we begin.

"Today," I say, "we are at Perkins in Edina, one of our favorite places to go, especially at night. I thought we would talk about friendships and how our illnesses affect them. So Benji, how did you interact with your friends before you got ill? What were your friendships like then?"

"*I had lots and lots of friends. I can't say that they were all close friends, but I was able to bounce around from friend to friend, and I was never bored. Everyone always wanted to be my friend, because I was always the class clown in middle school and in high school. Going into college, I was quickly labeled the party animal, because every Friday and Saturday I hit it hard."*

"And you had a lot of friends because you did that?" I ask.

"Yeah, it is the thing to do in college."

"You said they weren't all close. Did you have close friends?"

"Yeah," he says, *"I did, but I noticed before my illness I had a lot of problems with intimacy; in retrospect, even with my companions, I didn't ever let anyone in to know the real me. I don't know if deep down I was suppressing something or hiding something. However, every time someone was trying to get to know me, I would push them away and hurt them."*

I begin laughing. I can see that Benji is taking offense, but for some reason, I can't stop chuckling. "I'm thinking of the movie *Good Will Hunting*. We have Will Hunting here. Just kidding. So that was how you were before you were ill?"

"Yeah."

"And do you think that was just a stage you were going through, or did your illness change that."

"I think that because of my illness, my up-and-down moodiness, I was never stable enough to stay with a decision long enough. I would like a woman, but by the time I would ask her out, I didn't even want to date her anymore."

"The friends you had before you were ill, do you still have those friends today?"

"Some . . . some I don't."

"What happened to the ones you don't have?"

"*They're still out there on the party scene, living life in the fast lane, and not looking back.*"

"So you lost your friends because you no longer party?" I ask.

"*Well, I found myself buried in bars a lot of the time when I was healthy. Of course, I was probably unhealthy already, but I was undiagnosed. So I think I spent a lot of time using alcohol to compensate for my moods and caffeine to overcome my lows. Thus, basically I found that the people I hung out with at the bars kept on wanting to go to the bars; however, since I wasn't supposed to drink alcohol, I found going there too difficult. For a good period of time, I didn't want to give up these friends, so I would go to the bar and while on my medication, I would drink heavily.*"

Benji takes a drink of his decaf. "*It is kind of embarrassing, but I would pass out in all these weird places. I'd wake up in the morning and not know where I was, because I had passed out on some random floor or at some party. And that is not something I like to remember. So I had to decide either to give up the friends who weren't willing to hang out with me in an environment that was safe for me or continue the destructive path I was on. So I basically chose to forfeit those friends and keep the ones who were willing to work with me in different ways. And at the same time, I had to learn to have more . . . what is the word?*"

"Self control or self restraint," I suggest.

"*Self control and abstinence of alcohol—so that I could still go to the bar and order something like ginger ale without the Jameson or just order a glass of water. I always hated that bartenders would embarrass me when I ordered water by saying, 'What? You are only going to order water?' Also, I hated that I always had to explain to people why I didn't drink."*

"Is it hard to make new friends nowadays?"

"The place that most of my generation hangs out in is the bars and the nightclubs. I guess there are also the coffee shops. That is kind of what I replaced the bars with. But I can't drink caffeine, so even that is kind of an oxymoron. However, I have noticed that when I'm at a bar, I always have to explain why I don't drink, because they ask, 'Have you been through AA, or what is the deal?' If I try to be honest and tell them I'm on a medicine that I can't mix with alcohol, they ask more questions like, 'Oh, what do you have? Why do you take medicine?' And so, lately I've just been going with the staple response that I don't drink. It is a personal decision."

"And they don't question that?" I ask.

"No, instead they say, 'Oh, good for you.' Yet at the same time, if I explain that I used to drink and now I don't, it just leads to other questions. Ultimately, they're probably going to find out about my illness. When they do, they usually end the friendship."

"Okay, so when you do go out, either to the bars or the coffee shops, do you actually make new friends? Or is it hard for you?"

"At the bar," Benji says, *"I do not make friends very often. However, at the coffee shop, I'm having a lot of luck finding friends."*

I smile. "I'm not talking about girlfriends here; I'm just talking about friends."

"Yeah."

"People with a bipolar disorder are usually pretty charismatic."

"I think I'm charismatic in the way I talk to the barista at

Starbucks or any place like that."

"How has your illness affected friendships in the past?" I ask.

"*I just had to stop hanging out with a good number of kids in my fraternity during my senior year, because I couldn't do what they did three days out of the week—which was just drink. I found that I spent a lot of my senior year alone. That was hard for me. I'm in a better place now. In college everyone— unless you are part of Campus Crusade for Christ— drinks.*"

"How about nowadays? Does your illness affect your relationships with your friends now?"

"*To a certain extent yes,*" he says, "*but I have also learned how to manage it. I'm not striving to meet the same people in the same places as I was before. As far as the friends I already have, the ones who are close know what I'm going through, because I've told them, and they are open to helping me when I need help.*"

The waiter returns with Benji's club sandwich. He and I take a break while he eats, and then we start recording again.

"*Andrew,*" Benji asks, "*what were your interactions like with your friends before getting ill?*"

"In high school and before that, I only had three close friends. And that was about it. I didn't have lots of friends. However, the friendships I did have were very close. We hung out all the time and did everything together. Then I went off to college, and I didn't find anyone at Caltech who I was too close to. There were about six of us who all hung out together all the time. It is interesting that out of that group of six, one got schizophrenia (me), one had a brain tumor and died, and one has had like four strokes. Surprisingly, we are all in our young 20s and have had these serious brain problems. I find that interesting. At Caltech I started partying a bit; I never did in high school at all, and, as a result, I became quite popular at college. I mean I didn't consider anyone to be a real close friend, but I knew everybody. It is a small college, and I was friendly with everybody."

I prepare myself another coffee. "And then I went to Madison, when I left Caltech. All my friends from high school were there, and I thought it was going to be great. I got to go to a new school with all these old friends. However, they pretty much immediately stopped hanging out with me. I think one called me a couple of times to go lift weights, but I didn't have much motivation so I said I didn't want to go exercise. Then during the winter, I wanted to throw a little Super Bowl party at my place, but my friend said no, he couldn't come to the party. I stopped over at his place later only to discover that he was having a Super Bowl party and never invited me. So basically, they all pretty quickly abandoned me. I think it was because I was already starting to become a little bit weird. That might be the reason. I don't know any other reason."

I wasn't that sick then, so I don't know if I was that weird then. It is sort of a mystery to me. I continue. "When I went to Iowa State I had no friends, except my sister and her husband, who was her fiancé at the time. We hung out a little bit, but my sister stopped because she thought my weird actions might embarrass her in front of her friends.

"I spent most of the time at Iowa State and Madison by

myself completely. Actually, I did have one friend at Madison. I thought he was working for the CIA. Regardless, I was friends with him, because he was a cool guy, and I liked him a lot, even though I thought he was plotting against me. He was a nice guy, so we were still friends. We played tennis together and smoked a lot of cigarettes. And drank a lot of coffees."

"*You mentioned that a lot of these friends had left you. Do you have any of these friends still today? If not, what happened to them?*"

"I don't have a single friend from before I was ill," I say. "Not one."

"*That's astonishing.*"

"Yeah. And what happened to them? They are in med school and in PhD programs and all doing well. I think some of them might live here in the Twin Cities. I saw one friend one day down by the U getting on a bus, and he didn't want to talk to me. I have no idea. They just all stopped talking to me."

"*On the flip side for you, now that you don't have any of these friends, do you find that it is a lot harder to make new friends?*"

"I find it incredibly hard to make new friends. Part of it is that we are in Minnesota perhaps, because people in Minnesota aren't as friendly as in Madison, where they are pretty friendly. A lot of it is because of my illness. Because I don't read and I don't watch TV, I'm incredibly boring, and so I have nothing to talk to people about. Also, I'm pretty hard to get along with, I think. I don't know. I'm just a little bit weird, so that turns people off. Of course, part of it is my paranoia. For example, when I was a student at the U of M—this was after I was in treatment—I met this guy and we talked a few times and were in the same class together. It looked like we were going to be great friends. He was a cool guy. Like me, he was older—older than you were supposed to be in school, and he said it was because he was in the Navy. Immediately, my paranoia is thinking, 'Office of Naval Intelligence.' Therefore, I couldn't be his friend, because I thought he was a spy. So I have a hard time being friends with people I have paranoid thoughts about. This problem makes it tough making new friends, because any time I meet new people I get suspicious of them. So generally I try not to meet new people."

Before I met Benji, I was friendless for a few years. I can't even describe how lonely I felt back then. It was horrible. The loneliness was exacerbated by the fact that I tend to isolate myself socially when I'm not feeling very well, and in those times I was quite ill.

I think I isolate myself to reduce the stress of my environment. When I'm around too many people, I feel a bit unsettled and uncomfortable, and the best way to relieve those feelings is to isolate myself. Even now when my family throws a party, I have to excuse myself continuously from the party to reduce my stress, lest I become symptomatic again. The guests never understand this and think I'm being asocial.

Due to my illness, I have become an introvert, and I prefer my own company to that of almost anyone. It is rejuvenating for me to be alone, and if I don't have enough alone time during the day, I become symptomatic. Since I live with my parents, neither of whom works, much of my time alone is late at night. As such,

I tend to stay up late so that I can have enough time by myself to relax before I go to bed. I always need that time, and it is my favorite time of the day.

I take a drink of my coffee, and I see that Benji is about to ask me something serious.

"*Have you ever had suspicious thoughts of me?*" he asks.

"Not yet," I say and begin laughing.

"*That's odd.*"

"Not yet. I've never had suspicious thoughts about my sister either. It just depends on the person."

Even if I did have paranoid thoughts about Benji, I would never admit them to him. If I ever had paranoid thoughts about a friend, and he found out about them, I'm pretty sure that would put an end to the friendship. Paranoia can even put an end to committed marriages, and so I wouldn't think twice about the possibility of my paranoia ending a friendship.

I turn the recorder off, and we finish a couple more cups of coffee and head out.

CHAPTER 16:
ROMANTIC RELATIONSHIPS

We're back at my parents' house in the spa room. It is early afternoon, and Benji just finished with classes for the day. I have my usual Diet Cherry Coke, and he has his caffeine-free Diet Coke. I'm rocking in my chair, and Benji is pacing a bit in the room. I turn the recorder on and we begin.

"All right," I say, "today is Good Friday, so Easter is coming up in a couple days. Today we are going to talk about how our illnesses have affected our romantic relationships. Before you were ill, I would like to know a little bit about your romantic efforts, like how did they work out for you?"

"Well, the truth is they didn't work out very well before I was ill, and while I was ill, my efforts were pretty haphazard. Yet, now that I'm ill, and I know I'm ill, my romantic endeavors are getting better."

"It's getting better now that you are ill?" I start laughing. "Is that what you're saying?"

Benji starts laughing too. "*I don't know. I think I was on and off with symptoms for so long—like the last 10 years of my life, ever since my freshman year in high school—that any woman I have gone after has told me that I'm too unpredictable and too unstable.*"

"How were you unpredictable or unstable? What do you mean by that? Or what did they mean by that?"

"*I don't know what they meant by that,*" Benji says. "*It ticks me off. I would fall head over heals manically in love with women and feel obsessed with them. By the time I finally shared that I was interested in them, I expected the world, but they would hardly know me. Sometimes, I was already friends with the woman, but she wasn't ready to jump into a romantic relationship. I once gave a picture frame to a woman for her birthday, a picture of us. Behind the picture, I wrote a poem about how much I yearned for her. Finally, I called her up one night to ask her out. And she said, 'Ahh, I'm kinda interested in this other guy.' And I answer, 'Yeah, why don't you look behind the picture frame and read the poem I wrote you?' After she read the poem, she started sobbing on the phone and asked why I didn't tell her months earlier when things might have been different, because now we were such good friends. This is one example of how part of me was always too afraid to get too close to people. I became good friends with a lot of women, but since I never was able to share deep emotions, I rarely managed to develop intimate relationships with any of them. Therefore, I internalized a lot of pain.*"

"And that was all before you were diagnosed?" I ask.

"*Before I was diagnosed. I guess going after woman after woman every night when I was manic, in the height of my mania, was part of my symptoms. After I was diagnosed, however, I found it hard to meet any women, partially because my self esteem was so low. Also, I couldn't look in my normal places, the clubs and the bars, because I wasn't drinking anymore. For the same reasons, it was difficult to make new friends; any time the question of alcohol came up, I had to say I'm trying not to drink so much because I take medicine. This prompted them to ask, 'Oh, why do you take medicine?' They would be all intrigued to learn about my illness, but then once they discovered I was sick, they wanted to be my friend, but nothing more."*

"Right," I say, "they would never want to date you, it usually seems."

"Yeah."

"Where have you gone to meet women? Or how do you go about meeting them?"

"Now?"

"Yeah."

"Coffee shops," Benji says. *"That is why our conversations usually take place in the coffee shop, because we are usually looking for women. Am I right?"*

"Yeah, you're pretty much right. How is that working out for you?"

"So far it is working out all right."

"You met the barista at Starbucks."

"Yeah, I met the barista at Starbucks, but who knows what will happen with that relationship? I'm not going to get worked up."

"Sounds like a plan."

"With you, Andrew," Benji says, *"before you were diagnosed,*

where did you find your love interests, and how long did they last? With me, everything was sort of short, and I couldn't get intimate with anyone because I was always up and down emotionally with my moods, which made it difficult to share intimacy. How about with you?"

"I was almost the exact opposite. I didn't have that many relationships, but the ones I did have were generally very deep. For example, I dated a girl seriously in high school for about two years. She was my first love, and I still like her a lot. She is a great person. I have contacted her by e-mail a couple of times just to see how her life is turning out, and it seems she is doing well. So I'm happy about that. When I went to Caltech, I dated a young woman, again for about a year and a half to two years. And again, she is a wonderful person; I think she is married now and maybe has a child. That is the last I heard, but I'm not in contact with her now."

I take a drink of Diet Coke and continue. "I noticed that when I started becoming ill, while I was still dating my girlfriend at Caltech, I stopped having interest in the relationship. Becoming disengaged emotionally is one early symptom of schizophrenia. I just didn't care for her anymore. Furthermore, I didn't want to be around anybody, including her. So I stopped really caring for her and had no feelings for her, bad or good—just nothing. As a result, I totally stopped making an effort to keep up the relationship, and she broke up with me. Next, I met a woman while I was at Madison. Although she was really beautiful, I only stayed with her for about a month, because I thought she was working for the CIA and that she was in on this conspiracy against me.

One reason why I thought that she was spying on me was because she was so beautiful that I thought she was too good for me. A woman like that wouldn't be interested in me, so she must have ulterior motives for dating me. I'm not that cool, but this woman was knock-out, drop-dead gorgeous. So I started thinking she was working for the CIA. I never told her that, of course. We broke up after just a short period of time, like a month or six weeks. After Madison, I went to Iowa State and didn't date anyone there. I was still ill at the time."

I light a cigarette. "From Iowa State and after being in treatment for the mysterious mental health condition, I then went to the U of M. While there in December 2003 I went off my medications and lost a lot of weight. I became super confident. Consequently, I started dating a woman again. We dated for six months or so. However, I was off my meds at the time, and I started to get paranoid again about a lot of different things, even about her a little bit. I had a lot of trust issues, but I didn't bring it to her attention; they were just things that I internalized. My inability to trust led to problems in our relationship, like thinking she was cheating on me and stuff like that. It never went beyond my thoughts, but it still affected the relationship. She ended up leaving me when I was diagnosed. Since then I haven't had any women as girlfriends or whatever. I've made a lot of efforts, but none of them have worked out."

"*First of all,*" Benji asks, "*did the woman who broke up with you when you were diagnosed ever give you a reason for leaving?*"

"She never did, but she is with another guy now, or at least she was just after leaving me, so she could have left me for him.

However, I think the reason she left me for him is that, well, I would always tell her about what I was thinking, not the paranoia about her, but other things, about my hallucinations. I could see the hair on her arms would stand up, because she was so freaked out. So I let her into my crazy little world, and she got scared about it. It was just too overwhelming for her, which is a little unfortunate because I loved her a lot. She was scared about that, too, because my future was so unpredictable. Regretfully, I understand that she didn't want to hitch herself to my wagon, because who knows what my life would turn out to be?"

"And looking at your life now," Benji asks, *"why do you find it difficult to meet women?"*

"There are a lot of reasons. I will try to remember all of them. The first reason I have difficulty meeting women is where I live. There are not that many young girls here. I don't meet 20-something-year-old women every day. So it is hard. Also, for the past couple of years, I have been pretty much homebound, because I haven't driven much. The women are not going to show up in my room. Obviously, under these circumstances, I don't meet women that often. However, when I do meet them, I have a terribly tough time for several reasons."

I grab my Coke and take a drink. "One thing is that I don't have a job. The first thing they do is ask, 'What do you do?' If I don't have a job, I look like this big-time loser to them, and they, especially the women around here, want someone with a big-time career, making big-time bucks. Another strike against me is that I live at home. 'Where do you live?' is the second question. I tell them I live at home with my parents, and that is probably pretty loser-ish, too. Now that I am moving out to my own condo, maybe things will get better. Those are two reasons. A third reason is that, let's see, I'm weird. That's a big thing. I've become so weird with my illness, and women don't like weirdoes that much. Furthermore, I don't watch TV and I don't read, so I don't have that much to talk to them about. Currently, I don't have that many interests, and that is a change from the past. Having so few interests makes conversation near to impossible. I don't even like conversing with most people."

I take another drink and then set my Coke down. "This list is getting long. There were about five more things I had in my head. I'm forgetting them now. Basically, I consider my biggest drawback to be lacking the successful career. I believe I could find a woman if I had a career. I generally try to meet women anywhere I go, but mostly, it is the coffee shops."

Benji begins laughing. "*Anywhere you go?*"

"Anywhere I go. I spend much of my time at the coffee shop drinking coffees; however, that hasn't worked out yet. There was one woman who gave me her phone number about a week or two ago. I called her twice, but she never returned my calls. Obviously, she isn't interested, but I was excited for a short period of time. Being unable to develop meaningful relationships is disappointing. Once I give up on trying to find a woman, I'm generally okay in life; however, as soon as I get the idea that I can find someone, I get excited. Then, when it doesn't work out, I get bummed. As a result, I often feel I should just give up on trying to find a woman, because it is so difficult to find someone who will be okay with my diagnosis and my peculiar lifestyle and personality."

I think I have been trying too hard at finding a girlfriend. It always seems that when I'm looking for a girlfriend, I never find one, and when I'm not, I do. I've decided that I'll still go out and about and be open for whatever may happen, but I won't waste so much mental effort on these matters. At the moment, that approach seems to be the best way forward for me, and perhaps I'll get a date sometime soon.

I continue. "I have gone out on one date since I was diagnosed, pretty much. I met that woman at a fundraiser for an organization that helps the mentally ill. She already knew I had schizophrenia, but agreed to go out with me anyway. That date was with a very nice, very beautiful woman. We went out to dinner and a movie, and I paid for everything. I held her hand during the movie, and, when I went back to her place, I gave her a goodnight kiss. The kiss caused her to freak out on me." I start to chuckle. "Apparently, she did not consider this a date; instead, it was just friends going out. I thought it was a date. So it didn't work out, but we are friends now. I have a second friend, which is nice, because she is a nice person."

"*Second friend?*" Benji asks. "*Who is your first friend?*"

"You."

He laughs hysterically.

"So that is nice." I say, "I have a friend, even though the romantic relationship didn't work out. When I tried to date her,

I came across as this obsessed psycho. Understandably, she didn't like that."

While still laughing, Benji asks, "*What is the coincidence about both of your friends?*"

"Oh, both have bipolar. She has bipolar, also."

CHAPTER 17:
SOME THOUGHTS IV

In health class during high school we studied a unit on mental illness. I don't remember learning much about schizophrenia, only that people with it often hear voices. At the time I thought it would be cool to hear voices. I now know that it isn't. I don't remember talking about the stigma of mental illness, but I imagine that we must have. I know we didn't talk about the loneliness of mental illness, and as I sit here now with very few meaningful relationships, I think that would have been the most important thing to know.

To me, the loneliness of mental illness is immeasurable. I ache in my body for relationships with others, but virtually to no avail. I do have Benji's friendship; that has saved me in part from total dismay. But I still need a woman to share my life with. No matter how happy and content I become, I feel something is missing without a woman in my life.

I often wonder why I think I need a woman for completeness. Is it merely a biologically innate impulse, or is it God's plan for mankind? If it is God's desire for men to be united with women, then what good does it serve that I'm alone? Despite such questions, I know how I feel: I need a woman to share my life with.

Times of loneliness are often times of reflection, and in these periods I often ponder the meaning of life. What is the point of humanity's existence? Up until a few months ago, I would have said our purpose was to love and be loved, to foster loving relationships between people. But as I see it now, that idea is quite flawed: I can't control who loves me. So now, I have stricken out the idea of being loved. The point of our existence, it seems to me, is simply to love. In this new understanding, I don't need to have love in return. I can simply love others; it need not be reciprocal.

Accordingly, I have been trying to live my life with this new credo. It seems that I can have a purposeful life without the love of a woman. But that is still only an intellectual understanding that rests on the surface of my psyche, and what I need is an emotional understanding that reaches deep into my core.

This is analogous to the problem I was having reconciling my religious faith with my suffering. I had read some theological theories into the study of this problem, called theodicy, but they only made sense to my intellect. Emotionally, I was still suffering. To me, the theories were empty words. It is one thing to satisfy the intellect about suffering (or loneliness), but it is an entirely different thing to comfort someone who suffers (or is lonely). There is a human element involved to comfort, an element that transcends mere words.

I remember when I first went off to college to study at

Chapter 17: Some Thoughts IV

Caltech, the first thing I missed of home was my girlfriend's little tugs on my arm. It was the small affectionate touches that I missed. Without them, I felt empty, like I had become a robot that failed to truly feel. That robotic-like feeling became the norm for a while. Then, it came and went along with my future romantic endeavors.

Currently, that robotic-like feeling has returned; it has been with me for years. I still cannot get used to it. I forever remember the feeling of affection, and that memory reminds me that at least at one time, I was a person who knew the meaning of life—maybe not intellectually or even consciously, but emotionally. All I have now are my memories. But those memories continue to sustain me as I dream of something better.

CHAPTER 18:
FAITH

B enji and I have been hanging out nearly every day, but I haven't been in the mood to record. Today is Wednesday, and ever since last Sunday, I have been tired and unmotivated. Sunday was Easter, and it was a big letdown for me. My parents and my sister and her family were vacationing in Palm Springs, so I spent Easter with Benji; his parents were in Wisconsin, and he didn't feel like driving five hours to see them. My brother and his family came over in the early evening, and we all ate Easter dinner together.

I have been unmotivated, but today I am forcing myself by sheer willpower to get back to talking about my life with mental illness. This is one of my periods of lack of motivation. I haven't brushed my teeth in three days, and I have been worrying endlessly about getting cavities. The worry causes me distress, but not enough to get me to brush my teeth.

The spa room is cold today; therefore, I am sitting in the rocking chair wearing my winter jacket. I have my Diet Coke, and Benji has his caffeine-free Diet Coke. We are about to start recording, but Benji wants me to light a smoke before I begin. I assume it is because doing so has become a ritual that we go through when we talk about our mental illnesses. I finally light a smoke, and we begin.

"Today," I say, "is Wednesday, and there is a snowstorm outside. We are getting a lot of snow. We are at my parents' house, sitting in the spa room."

Benji corrects me. "*The winter garden.*"

"The winter garden. We are having the 13th of our recorded conversations. Today, Benji, I thought we would talk about faith a little bit. Would you describe your current faith, if you have one?"

"*Sure. I'd say overall I would consider myself a practicing Christian. I grew up in a Lutheran family that went to church regularly. I don't frequent church as much as I did growing up, but I still go from time to time.*"

"And you were confirmed in the Lutheran church and all that?"

"*Yeah,*" Benji says.

"Having become ill, has that affected your faith at all? Either more faith, less faith, or different faith?"

"*Well, while I was ill, when I was manic and unmedicated, I probably had no faith. I went for a long period of living faithlessly. When I was hospitalized, I was surrounded by people who were having problems with religious grandiosity. They thought I was a prophet, and before long I started to believe it.*"

Chapter 18: Faith

"So you started to believe that you were a prophet?"

"Yeah. I even thought I had healing powers. I was in such a sick place at the time, because the doctors had yet to find just the right combination of meds for me. I met this guy who told me I should read the book of Micah, because his name was Micah. The book of Micah alludes to Revelation. He had a picture drawn on a scrap piece of paper, and he said I should get it as a tattoo. He said, 'I know I drew this to give to someone, and you are the person who is going to get this tattoo.'"

"Did you get the tattoo?" I ask.

"No, I told him that I wasn't the right person for the tattoo. I thought I was like Neo, and I wasn't ready for it yet."

"Neo is from what movie?"

"The Matrix. Then there was a young woman who was pregnant at the hospital, and she thought I was supposed to marry her and claimed that I was the father of her baby, because she thought she had a holy baby. As all of this was going on in the hospital, the tsunami occurred in Sri Lanka. Everyone in the hospital who was in the lockdown unit watched as 100,000 people were killed by the tsunami. All they could think about was the story of Noah and his ark. They thought that somehow Revelation was close, which resulted in everyone, including me, having this heightened religiosity. My life became this kind of Bible code. I read through the Bible for a specific period after this, and I looked through the book of Micah. I also read all of Revelation. From these readings, I always tried to tie things in the Bible to my own life. For example, if you look at the book of Revelation, it has lots of numbers. The number 12 come up numerous times: I was born on the 12th of September, so, that *number was meaningful to me. And then the number 144 comes up a lot. And that is . . ."*

"Twelve squared," I say.

"Yeah. Also, I was in the hospital four years after 9/11, and four is a divisor of 12. Having my birthday one day after 9/11, I thought I was supposed to be the one to come down and bring peace. I read a lot about the tribe of Benjamin and who he was in the bible. The tribe of Benjamin and the tribe of Jacob were the two main tribes that made it through a war against all 12 tribes. These two tribes survived all the battles. Therefore, I thought that I was the modern-day Benjamin come to fight this new war against terror. My heightened religiosity came from the influence of the people around me in the hospital. I wasn't looking for it, but I was always looking for symbolism when I was manic, which eventually led me to look in the Bible for symbolism, and there is a lot of it in the Bible. You can find almost anything in the Bible and interpret it however you want."

"Do you still have those thoughts?" I ask.

"No."

"How did they go away?"

"Medicine," he says.

"Medicine. Okay. So what about now? Does that confuse your faith, having thought you were a prophet and now thinking you are not? Does that confuse your faith at all?"

"It did for a while. I remember my family pastor came to visit me in the hospital after I had been there for two weeks. I told him about all this weird stuff that was happening, and he didn't know what to say. He said, 'I hope you start feeling better.' Looking back,

I don't think there is much he could have said, because it was so inexplicable. Today I think I'm kind of back to where I was before I became ill. I don't want to become overly religious, because I have this fear that I will become hyperreligious again. I think I can have my beliefs, but I don't have to give away everything I have or try to change the world by going on some global quest. Those were the kind of dreams I was having at the time—that I should manage these large-scale changes. I'm just one person. Maybe I do have some big dreams, but I just want to live with my mortality for now. If there is something greater planned for me, I'm not opposed to it, but I have to question it a little bit now because I was sick at the time. And quite frankly, I just want to live a normal life."

"Does your faith help you cope with your illness at all?" I ask.

"Not really."

I'm slightly shocked. "That's an honest answer."

"The medicines help me the most, and the psychotherapy helps me more than religion. Religion is helpful, I think, but more for things outside of my illness. I think my illness is something I tweak with the medicines and psychoanalysis. When life issues come up that are more pressing or bigger than this, I turn to prayer. It is not that I blame anyone or that I blame God for this illness. Indeed, in retrospect, the bipolar disorder is one of the best things that has happened to me. Without it, I would never have had an appreciation for my true gifts, and I wouldn't have become as close or as honest with my family. After the death of my grandfather, which you will remember was the catalyst for the emergence of my illness, I developed a beautiful relationship with my grandma. When I'm

depressed I almost write prayers in the form of poems. I've written over 200 of them now, and I remember I wrote one about how my grandma saved me from Satan's grasp and led me to God's heavenly plan. Strangely enough, when I'm depressed, I write poems with religious themes. They are usually a prayer for peace and forgiveness, but I don't necessarily pray for myself. I'm not like, 'Cure me, cure me, cure me' but I'm like, 'Help me learn from where I am, and help me become a better person from all of this.'"

I turn off the recorder, and we take a five-minute break. I turn the recorder back on, and we begin again.

"Okay, Andrew," Benji says, *"what would you say your current faith is?"*

"I am a born-again Christian—a Bible-believing, God-fearing Christian. I go to and am a member of Wooddale Church in Eden Prairie. It is a multidenominational church; it is a member of, I guess, the Four Cs, which is the Conservative Christian Churches Conference or something like that, and also Baptist. It is the type of church where a lot of people raise their hands, like the Jewish people used to do while praying in the time of Jesus. So a lot of people raise their hands during the songs when they become emotional. I don't raise my hands, but I'm a very strong Christian. That is where my faith is right now."

"How about prior to being ill? Did you have any religious background at all?"

"Yeah," I say, "I grew up in a Lutheran church, like almost everybody in Minnesota."

Benji starts laughing.

I continue. "I was confirmed in a Lutheran church and went through confirmation. I was baptized as an infant. Yet I never believed. I did it because it was what you do, but as beliefs go, I had none. I didn't feel it; I didn't think it. Toward the end of high school I was at best agnostic; I didn't know if there was a God or not. At worst, I would have considered myself an atheist, because most of the time I believed there was no God. It wasn't that I was uncertain; it was that I believed no God existed. Then I went to Caltech, and my atheist belief was reinforced, because I became big into biology, evolution, and a naturalistic worldview. Therefore I thought, 'Of course there is no God. People who think there is a God must be idiots.' I did know a lot about the Bible, though. I read a lot about Christianity so that I could know how to refute it. As a result, when I had debates with people, I could usually win, because I was so good in philosophy. I still am. I could win any debate against any Christian, because most of them weren't educated Christians—at least the ones I met. These Christians were younger, they hadn't studied the Bible, and they hadn't studied Christian apologetics (which deals with the the systematic defense of Christianity). So I could win any argument with them about the validity of their beliefs. I did this quite a bit, but I didn't go to the point of being against God. I would let people believe in what I considered to be a delusion, because I realized it helped them cope with the stresses of life. I didn't actively try to wreck anyone's faith."

I take a drink of my Diet Coke. "My girlfriend at Caltech also was an atheist. Her parents were very strong atheists. Her parents and I didn't get along at all; it was really bad. I always encouraged my girlfriend to be her own person, to be an adult and to make her own decisions about things. And out of that encouragement came her yearning for God. Basically, she wanted to know who this Jesus of Nazareth was and what was he about. I encouraged her to explore faith, even though I thought it wasn't true. We read the Bible together a little bit, and we watched the movie *Jesus of Nazareth*. I told her what I had learned growing up and in my private studies, and she became a Christian. It was like I witnessed to her, and her parents hated me for that. They thought I was a Bible-thumping Christian forcing their daughter to become Christian so I could control her mind. All the while I was a major atheist, which is funny. I was there when she got baptized. Today she is a strong Christian, and I don't think her parents like that a bit. Many times we would meet with this pastor of a Lutheran church in Pasadena, Calif., and ask him questions about Christianity, and the more we talked the more convinced I was that it wasn't true. And so I left Caltech with my atheism still intact. I held to those beliefs until I started becoming ill."

I set my Coke down on the coffee table. "When I started becoming ill, I had this need for faith. I started praying for God to come into my life, because I would see Christians who were having fun and loving life. Well, I was ill and suicidal and hated life. I just wanted to die. I wondered how these Christians could be so happy when this world is so horrible and evil and bad. I wanted God to come into my life, but nothing seemed to happen. However, after I was in treatment for schizophrenia, I started to read a lot of philosophy and Christian apologetics. I had read them all before, but I wanted to refresh my memory. Suddenly I found all the arguments convincing. The proofs for or against the existence of God aren't

100 percent. You either agree with them or you don't, but they don't provide 100 percent proof. Yet suddenly I started agreeing with all these things. When I started getting ill, I finally realized something: The wisdom I gained from my illness was that humans have inherent worth. I wouldn't have agreed with that before I was ill. I would have thought that you make your own worth through contributions to society. Before my illness, I believed myself to be a stellar person with potential to contribute to society in great ways. But when I got this illness, I felt that I would be a bum the rest of my life. Then I realized that my worth didn't change—I was still the same person with the same worth. This realization certainly didn't fit my atheistic worldview. Thankfully, I started seeing these arguments for God to be convincing, and I started believing in God."

I light a cigarette and continue. "I went on a quest exploring different religions and came to the conclusion that Christianity is true. So I invited Jesus into my heart. What convinced me most that Christianity is true is something I had read in an apologetics book: there was a historical Jesus who is mentioned outside of the Bible. He did exist and was crucified and all that. The next debate in my mind was whether this historical Jesus was God. What convinced me on this point was that the people who knew him best then—his apostles—knew whether he was God or a fraud, or even crazy like I am. All of them who were in direct contact with him, except for John, died martyrs' deaths. Religious zealots commonly died for their faith throughout history, but they only died for a faith they believed to be true. No one dies for a lie. Surely then, all these people knew whether or not Jesus was the true God. They all were willing to die for their faith, so it must have been true. That was my reasoning, so I invited

Jesus into my heart and became a Christian. I even got baptized by full immersion last summer. That is where my faith is now."

"*Does your faith help you cope with your illness?*" Benji asks.

"I think so. It has in the past big time, but I'm wondering if it does anymore, since I'm doing so well. The big thing is that I tend to get hopeless, and I start getting suicidal. I get hopeless because I think that things won't change. The thing about my faith is that when I realize that God does love me and will take care of my needs, I don't get hopeless. Romans 8:28 says, 'And we know that in all things God works for the good of those who love him, who have been called according to his purpose.' So I know that in all things God will take care of me and work for my own good. That helps me accept the things that are going bad in my life, and it keeps me from getting hopeless. Because of my faith, I can keep up hope in those dark moments."

"*Many people with schizophrenia,*" Benji says, "*have problems with hyperreligiosity and religious delusions. Have you had any of those?*"

"Yeah. A lot. That is part of my problem. I think I come across as this religious nut, because a lot of times in the past I've been one step away from preaching on a street corner somewhere. When this started about a year ago or so, I was in church and started getting messages from God. They weren't auditory, like voices. They were, instead, what is called a delusion of reference, which is when you take things in the environment and think they have a personal, significant meaning to you. For example, some people watch TV and think that a news anchor is talking directly to them. My delusion of reference occurred when the pastor was giving a sermon in church. I determined that the sermon was just for me. He was speaking directly to me, and I thought I was supposed to become like Moses and be a professional speaker and evangelist. Now, my number-one fear in life is public speaking. I cannot do it. Subsequently, Moses had this same fear. He said, 'I can't speak, I'm not articulate.' And God said that he would give him the words. That is what it was like with me. I thought I was supposed to be like Moses and start public speaking. I have had the opportunity to speak publicly because of my work with the Barbara Schneider Foundation. When I was asked to start speaking, I thought, 'This is weird, because I had this message from God to speak, and they are now asking me to speak,' so I have to do it. I hated it, but I had a lot of success. I was doing something I thought I couldn't do, because I thought God was helping me. And then, I was in my room one night, and God communicated messages to me again, or at least that is what I thought. The thoughts were that I should start a ministry of my own, a mental illness ministry at my church. So I went about starting it, and it is still up and running. This ministry is a program of support groups and presentations. The program is getting popular, and many people love it. However, I started the ministry not because I wanted to but because I thought God told me to and I had to do it."

I finish off my Coke and snuff out my cigarette. "I've also seen angels in hallucinations, and demons. I've seen Jesus. So I have a lot of problems with religion. While I was getting these messages from God, my faith went through the roof; I would have died for it. As a result, the world changes somehow. Before, when I had a naturalistic worldview, the world was only atoms and forces, and it was blah. But now I live in this world haunted by spirits, which is far more interesting. I am empowered to think I can do anything because God is on my side. So I have this hyperreligiosity."

When I have paranoia, I can usually tell that it is only a product of my illness. I've had it for so long, and I'm always on guard against it. Such wasn't the case with my hyperreligiosity. It came on so slowly that I couldn't detect that a change from normal, or if I did detect a slight change, I thought it was a normal one, like spiritual growth, and not madness.

"Benji," I say, "it came to my attention that these weren't real messages the day when you and I stayed up all night in my room a few months back. I talked aloud about my thoughts, and I never tell anyone my thoughts. Through the process of voicing my own thoughts, I realized that I'm really sick: God hadn't been talking to me. That realization was a crushing blow. I had another one a couple of weeks later, when I realized that my hyperreligiosity wasn't real. As a result, my faith has been hurt a lot. I still have the intellectual beliefs, but I've lost my passion for things religious. Furthermore, I haven't been to church for a little while now, in part because I don't have the concentration to last through a whole service. But another part of it is that my passion is dying off. However, the last couple of days it has been up again. I'm feeling good about that. I've been listening to Christian rock, and the music helps me get in the mood to love Jesus."

CHAPTER 19:
WORK

I had to go to the eye doctor yesterday to get a prescription for new contacts. I had been dreading the appointment all morning long, but at the last minute, I decided to go. When I arrived, I discovered that it was a pediatric clinic. They said it was okay for me to be there, even though I'm 26 years old. I felt uncomfortable, but at least I got to color a picture with crayons. Well, maybe I didn't actually do any coloring, but I might as well have. The important thing was that I made it through the appointment okay, and I will have new contacts delivered to my house in about a week or so.

I absolutely hate going to doctors. It always seems that I go to the doctor feeling fine, and I come out with some horrific diagnosis and quite a bit of pain. I understand the ridiculousness of my thinking, and I know that I will have these terrible illnesses independent of doctors' diagnoses. Yet I can't help but associate doctors with pain and torment. I group dentists in with doctors, and in my estimation, they are the worst. The only doctors I don't mind, and actually like, are psychiatrists.

While half of all psychiatrists are truly below average in talent, the good ones are not only vitally important, but also fun to see. Unlike other doctors, the psychiatrist's job is to make you feel as good as possible at all times. While psychologists haven't been all that helpful for me, they are similarly committed to making you feel good and are delightful to see. For some reason, psychiatrists and psychologists always seem to like things about me and quite readily point them out. In therapy, I have learned that I have beautiful eyes and that I'm also quite a snappy dresser. They apparently like my shirts a lot. All kidding aside, despite the saccharine compliments, they make a world of difference in helping me become content.

I'm making my way back into the spa room of my parents' house, and Benji is with me. We have our Cokes, my regular and his decaf, and we are set to begin. I turn my recorder on and set it on the table.

"Today," I say, "is Friday the 13th and..."

"*Ooooh.*"

"Perhaps this will go badly today. We are having our 14th conversation about our lives. It is a little after 8 at night, and we are at my parents' house in the winter garden. I thought we would talk a little bit concerning our dreams about careers and our aspirations. Benji, when you were young, say, high school age or before college, what did you want to do for an occupation?"

"*That is kind of interesting. When I was in elementary or middle school, I always wanted to be an architect.*"

CHAPTER 19: WORK

"What kind of architect? Did it matter?"

"*I wanted to design airports,*"he says, "*but there weren't a lot of airports being built those days. Nevertheless, I liked drawing, but at some point that dream kind of died. I forced myself to be more like my father: He was in finance, wore a monkey suit to work, and flew all over the world making big deals. I thought I had to do that to make him proud. So I gave up my dream of being an architect. But ever since I became ill, I have rethought everything I dreamed of doing, such as being in international business and traveling around the world. I do not think I could handle the stress these jobs would create. According to my doctor and my parents and myself, especially myself, I don't think I could handle the stress involved with a corporate job that would be so demanding. It isn't that being an architect isn't demanding, because it sure as hell is demanding, but this career utilizes my creativity. What I realized through my mania is that I'm extremely creative. When I had my first case of mania, it brought back all my childhood memories of what I used to love. I started drawing and writing in a journal. I would draw in it and write in crayon. I was doing all these things that were creative to me but psychotic to other people. You shouldn't write legal documents in red crayon and bring it to your law professor. Soon after I did that, I was hospitalized.*"

"You thought you were being creative," I say, "and they thought you were being psychotic. Do you still have all those journals now?"

"*Yeah.*"

"Looking back on it now, do you think they are creative or that they are psychotic?"

"*Both. These journals are definitely a sign of my psychosis, because I was paranoid that people were going to steal my creative ideas. I thought my ideas were so creative and innovative that if other people touched them, they might copy them or take credit for the work that I had done. That's why I wrote a contract to protect my intellectual property.*"

"When did you realize that you couldn't handle the stress of a corporate job?"

"*At the very beginning, the summer before I went into my hypomania. The six months leading up to me being sent home from school, I kept telling my friends that I would never have a desk job. I had begun my ongoing quest to start my own business.*"

"Did you think it was too much stress at that time," I ask, "or was it that you just didn't want to do it?"

"*I didn't want to work in an office environment,*" Benji says. "*If it is stress I put on myself, it is okay. This self-imposed stress is good stress. However, if it is stress pushed upon me by my boss, my parents, law enforcement, etc, then . . .*"

I break out laughing. "Law enforcement?"

Benji starts laughing too, but continues his remarks. "*I don't like that stress. I wanted to start that international consulting firm because that is where my mind was at the time. I had just returned home from Asia, and I liked it so much that I wanted to go back there. Coming up with that international consulting firm business was an excuse to get me back to Asia. To this day, I still have all these big business ideas, but now they concern architecture, to change the industry and how things are done.*"

"The problem," I say, "is trying to tell the difference between a dream and a grandiose delusion. You talked about it before and said you couldn't tell."

"I'll go out on a limb here and say a lot of dreams are grandiose. Whether you're manic and have the illness I have, or whether you are Joe or Suzy out there in Smallville with the big dream. Maybe dreams are grandiose, but we prevent ourselves achieving them because people tell us we can't. Today, I'm not going to stop taking my medicines so that I can pursue my dreams. However, I used to think that medicines were preventing me from pursuing them. When I would get on the medicines, I would get more depressed and lack motivation. However, I have found that if the dream is strong enough, I can do it, even on the medication. Now every time I have a good idea I tell my dad, because if I ever start a business he will probably be my biggest investor or my manager or at least my financial advisor. My new goal is to be an architect."

"A landscape architect?" I ask.

"Yeah. A landscape architect, because I like gardening. I have a love for horticulture and plants. Even though I'm probably set back another four years to become the architect I want to be, it is funny to think that I'm healthy enough even to go to graduate school."

"Funny how? Like you don't think you are healthy enough to go to school?"

"It is weird that I am healthy enough to consider it," Benji says. *"I saw my doctor yesterday, and he said it was a great proposition and that he would totally support it. But a year ago, he would have been iffy about it; two years ago, he didn't even think I should go back to college to finish up my undergraduate degree."*

"Two years ago, would you have thought this was possible?"

"No. I'm living my loftiest dream in thinking that I'm overcoming this illness in a lot of ways."

I can see that Benji is living the dream. It is incredibly difficult to survive mental illness, let alone thrive with one. He is doing both, and I couldn't be happier for him.

He turns to me and says, *"Andrew, for you, I know that you are a smart individual . . ."*

"Thank you."

"And I have always looked up to you as very intelligent when it comes to math and science and stuff like that. I know you have said that you wanted to be a scientist. Is that what you wanted to be when you were young?"

"Yeah," I say, "When I was young, I wanted to be a doctor, but almost everybody wants to be a doctor when they are young. By the time I reached high school, my interests had changed. All through school, I was good in math and science. I was good at everything, pretty well rounded, but math and science came the easiest to me and I enjoyed them. My whole idea was to understand the world. I didn't know it at the time, but I was really philosophical. I didn't know what philosophy was then, but I knew I had a curiosity about how things worked. I would go on car trips up north and camping with my father. In his attempt to explain why the grass is green, or why the sky is blue, he would discuss science and physics a lot. It intrigued me, and I wanted to know about the world. So when I reached high school and took science classes, I quickly decided that I wanted to be a scientist.

CHAPTER 19: WORK

I wanted to make a discovery, or many discoveries. I wanted to explain the nature of the universe to people, because I thought it was so mysterious."

"So then, you went off to Caltech. That is one step you took to finding this path. And I think you continued to keep the dream through college, but did your dream change at any point?"

"Yeah," I say, "it did. I got disillusioned with science at Caltech."

"Why was that?"

"I think it was because of my illness. Suddenly at Caltech, I decided that I was going to be a writer—out of nowhere. I didn't have any training as a writer; I hadn't really taken any classes in writing. I got disillusioned with science because when I got into the thick of it, into the minutia of the nitty-gritty, I was losing the view of the forest for the trees. I wanted to change things on a bigger level. I didn't want to sit in a lab in a subbasement looking at spectrums of particles colliding. I wanted to make changes to the whole world in how humanity relates to nature. So I became disillusioned with science and decided to be a writer. Perhaps the reason I decided to become a writer can be found in the enjoyment I derived from writing in my journal, working on an assignment for a poetry class I was taking at the time. I continue to journal to this day, that obsessive journaling. I think it is called graphomania, being a compulsive writer. What I write isn't always meaningful; often it is like jumbled garbage. I do it today, and I write almost 10,000 words a day of garbage, because I'm a compulsive writer due to my illness."

My graphomania is probably the reason why I will be able to write as a career. Most things I have little or no motivation to do, but I have found that, even when I'm at my sickest, I still write compulsively. Slowly, I am trying to change over from this graphomania garbage writing to real prose.

I continue. "When I went to Madison, I couldn't get into the writing classes. After a period of time at home in Minnesota and before I went to Madison, I was out of science. I soon realized that I missed and loved science. At Madison I started reading all my old science textbooks from Caltech. I had a tendency at this time to buy books. Anytime I was bored I would go to the bookstore and buy a textbook. As a result, I have 60 or 70 textbooks on math and science. I would spend my time reading them because I thought they wouldn't teach me enough at Madison. I always had this dream of being a scientist, and then it went away, only to come back again. My passion has always been to understand the world. Accordingly, I am interested in philosophy, too. I read a lot of philosophy."

"*When did things change with your ability to achieve this dream?*" Benji asks. "*Is it still there, or has your dream of becoming a scientist been abandoned?*"

"It has pretty much passed. After I got onto the meds, I went back to the University of Minnesota and started to major in physics. I found out—surprise, surprise—that I couldn't solve physics problems anymore unless they were extremely easy. I took a class that covered the same material I learned as a freshman at Caltech, and I simply couldn't solve the problems. Also,

I took a math class, and I couldn't solve the math problems. A lot of people think that math is methodological: You apply a method or an algorithm, and you can solve the problem. Well, that may be true of derivatives, but not of integrals. Integrals are more of an art form. You need insight and a vision of how to solve the problem before you can solve it, and that is completely gone in me. So I can't solve physics and math problems very well anymore—certainly not in the time it takes to take a test in class. So I had to give up my dreams of being a scientist."

"What is your occupational goal now?"

"To be a writer," I say, "When I became ill, I realized that I have a lot of disabilities. One is that I'm bad at relating to people. I'm just not good with people. Also, I will have these periods of being sick when I can't work. So I thought the best career for me would be to become a freelance computer programmer or to be a writer. I hate computer programming. I'm decent at it, but I don't like it. So I thought I'd try my hand at writing. I enjoy it, and it is one thing I can do. As I go along in life, I'm finding that there are actually very few things that I can do. Since writing is one of the things I can do, I might as well choose to be a writer."

CHAPTER 20:
COPING

Tomorrow some professional window washers are coming to clean the windows on my parents' house. I hate when people are in the house, and I feel uncomfortable when they are in my room. I used to hate people coming into my room, and I didn't let anyone up there. Although I'm less paranoid now, I still don't like people in my room, in part because it is a total disaster area. I haven't picked it up in months and months, and now that these workers will be in my room, I have to clean it. So for the last day or so, I have been cleaning around the clock. It tires me out so that I have to take a break every 10 minutes; I'm not working on it that hard, but it is a large task that is taking up much of my time. The pressure to finish by tomorrow morning is causing me quite a bit of stress too.

I decide to stop cleaning for the moment, and invite Benji over for another conversation about our lives with mental illness. He arrives, we grab our Cokes, and head to the spa room. I take out my recorder and turn it on.

"All right," I say, "today is Sunday. We are recording our 15th conversation about our lives, about our mental illnesses, and about our unique struggles. Today I thought we would talk about coping with illnesses. Benji, you mentioned that medicines are important to you in controlling your symptoms, but that they are not a cure. You don't have the same life you had or would have had had you not become ill. So how do you cope with having a changed life?"

"*It is a question I can't fully answer,*" he says, "*because who can say what my life would amount to prior to my illness, as opposed to what my life is like now? In a lot of ways, coping isn't that hard. I had different potential prior to my illness. However, although the illness' limitations restrict me in some ways, in other ways, knowing your limitations allows you to seek things within your boundaries. When you don't have limitations, you think you can do anything. Maybe you can, maybe you can't. Being bipolar just made my limitations more visible to me. Before my illness materialized, I had limitations, but I didn't know about them. Therefore, I have limitations outside of my illness. My illness is just one of my limitations.*"

"You would rather know your limitations than have this false sense of being able to do anything?"

"*Before, I thought: 'What is going to stop me from being a billionaire? What is going to stop me from marrying Heidi Klum? Why can't I have a Ferrari?' That stuff is all intangible. Well, it is like conspicuous consumption. Now my limitations are what I can do with my career, what I can do socially. There are certain environments that I can't be around for the good of my health. Yet at the same time, knowing my limitations allows me to embrace the things that are still available to me, and that have more merit."*

I understand what Benji has been talking about, because my doctor told me the same thing. He said that everyone has limitations, and he acted like it was no big deal. For me, however, it was—and still is—a big deal. I can tell in many respects what my life would have been like had I not developed schizophrenia. Perhaps that is why I initially had such a hard time coping with my illness.

Benji's view seems correct, but I haven't met many people with mental illness who have similar views, and I ask him about it.

"I can't tell what my life would have been like," he says. *"I have only been through one crisis due to the illness. I'm only 24 years old. Maybe 20 years from now, when I'm 44 and have been through many crises and all sorts of awful things that can happen in mania and depression, my view will be different. I might be more jaded. But I think that if I take my medicine; I don't drink alcohol; stay away from caffeine; and have a good relationship with my doctor, caretakers, and my family and friends, I can be proactive about living with the illness, instead of letting it rule my life. So I have to make amendments in how I live, but in being proactive I can curb the ups and downs of my illness. I can call my doctor if I haven't slept for a few nights, and see him that week. Some people only get to see their psychiatrist once every three to six months, because that is all their insurance will cover, but I see mine every month for an hour and sometimes more. So in a lot of ways, I can cope because I have very good insurance and can afford*

the professionals who help me cope. As weird as it sounds, being born into a family that can afford to take care of my illness is probably the thing that helps me cope the most. I'm not working right now because my parents can afford to take care of me. If I had to get a job right now, it might be stressful on me. It's not that I'm not willing to work ever; it is just that I have to find a job with a stress-free environment. Also, my parents can afford a psychiatrist who doesn't deal with HMOs, and they can afford for me to see him one to two times a month. That is expensive."

"I have met a lot of people with mental illness," I say, "and a lot of them seem rather unhappy and discontent. But you are not one of them. You seem rather happy and content. How do you stay that way despite the fact that you have a severe and persistent mental illness?"

Benji begins to laugh. *"Well, when I'm depressed, I'm not content."*

"I don't mean symptoms of your illness like depression. I'm talking about when you are not going through symptoms, not in mania and not in depression, but in the middle, you are content. A lot of people are not content when they are not symptomatic. A lot of normal people are not content. How do you stay content, when you have this illness that affects all aspects of your life?"

"I think I am content because I have hope that I'll be able to acquire a piece of the American dream. To me, the biggest part of the American dream is overcoming adversity. You see so many immigrants who have to overcome all these hurdles to become citizens and to make it and become contributing members of society. I don't want to be a drain on society, because that is how I feel sometimes. A lot

of people think that people with mental illness are drains on society because they can't live productive lives. The contributions to society can come in a lot of different shapes and sizes, and I still have a lot of gifts to give, a lot of things bottled up inside of me that many people don't know about. I think I can make a difference in the world. Just by sharing how I feel about mental illness, I hope to help other people. When I was first experiencing mental illness, I was pretty depressed. However, the sad thing is that my mom was even more depressed than I was. She said, 'You're a bum now.' My dad has always been optimistic that I can overcome these hurdles that I face. So I'm always looking for something new that I can face, a challenge to overcome. Giving up the triggers that push me to the edge is probably about 90 percent of what has helped me stay healthy, and the other 10 percent is just the will to want to be better, to live healthfully. I deal with the mental illness in that everyone has a unique struggle, and this is my struggle. I will live as best I can with the gifts God has given me."

"You seem to keep up this hope quite well," I say, "that you are going to achieve a piece of the American dream and are going to overcome adversity. Does psychotherapy help you keep up this hope at all?"

"Yeah. I have a psychotherapist. He has always told me that I can pretty much accomplish anything I want. And, there have been a lot of people with my illness who have accomplished great things. So many of the impressionist painters were bipolar, and . . ."

"Musicians, actors, poets," I say.

"There is a long list of accomplished people with bipolar. I sometimes think that people who don't have my illness have tunnel vision. Normal people see the world through the emotions they experience,

but I feel emotions that are heightened to a point where I get 100 percent higher on both sides of the spectrum, and I experience more than what a normal person could. When I write poetry, I feel such deep emotion."

"If you met someone who was just developing bipolar and was having trouble coping, what would you tell him or her?"

"Well, it took me about two years to learn to cope. Feel free to share with close friends why you have to do certain things to stay healthy. A lot of normal people have a misconceived notion that taking the pills and taking the precautions of not drinking caffeine and alcohol are not necessary. However, they may only know people who take very mild dosages of anti-depressants; therefore, it doesn't matter much with their mild illnesses. With bipolar disorder, especially type one, which is the more severe form with larger up and down swings, your life is significantly changed. It isn't that you are just a little sad or happy every now and then. Your life is going to be different than other people's lives, and you have to make changes that aren't only mean-ingful but are safe. Too many people with this illness are homeless or suicidal. Luckily for me, I haven't experienced any of that yet. If I were to go off my meds, that outcome could certainly be possible. Too many people with bipolar think that once they are feeling better, they can stop taking the medicine. Of course, they relapse. But you need the medicine the most when you are feeling the best, because you know it is making a difference."

He pauses to take a drink and then continues. *"I had thought, up to three months ago, that as I feel better I could step down my medicine. I always had this idea that taking less meant that I was more normal. Then it got to the point where I started to get manic again, and I told my doctor that I needed to go back up to the full dose. Ever since then I've had the best three to four months, even including prior to my illness. These are the best three to four months I have experienced in years, and this is with the illness. I'm not saying that I don't go through times that are extremely difficult and trying and not fun, but if I can live 95 percent of the time in the middle, where I'm not experiencing such highs and lows, and I can take that other 5 percent and just manage that, there is where I want to be."*

Benji and I take a five-minute break, and then I turn the recorder back on.

"Andrew," he says, *"as things go, the two of us are probably the happiest mentally ill people—at least of those living in Minnesota right now."*

He begins laughing, and I do too.

"Yeah, probably," I say.

"At least in Edina, the suburb we are in right now. Living with schizophrenia is a serious, life-changing event that doesn't go away. It progressively gets worse as you get older, correct?"

"I think it gets progressively worse the first five years or so and then stabilizes. But, I'm not sure. It will become progressively worse if you don't take your meds."

"Somehow through all this turmoil, and all the letdowns you have experienced in your life, you seem to have a smile on your face and be happy and just in general find a way to be content with your situation. How do you do it?"

"I think it comes from my faith. I'm honestly thankful for

almost everything in my life. When I was sick, I went through hell, pretty much—at least it was the worst I have experienced in my life, and it gave me some perspective on life. Thus, I found faith. I started realizing that the things that were good in my life, which were very few (at least I thought they were few), were gifts from God. Then I started realizing I still had a lot of good things in my life. It was just that I had been feeling down, and I could only focus on the things that society thinks are important, like having your own children, which I probably won't ever have—at least the statistics say I won't have any—or having a meaningful career, which I probably won't have either. But I have a family that cares for me, and I have two friends. Any time I want to eat, I have food. I think about where I am in the scale of time. My life is basically better than a king's life in the 1600s. I literally walk around thinking about that. I think about how much more fortunate I am than some orphan born in Africa with AIDS. I think about that all the time, too, and that makes me thankful for what I have. I don't measure myself up to other people and say they have better lives than I do, that the grass is greener on the other side. I just look at my life and say, 'I have it good, and God has blessed me.'"

I actually feel guilty much of the time, because while I know that I'm blessed by God beyond belief, I also know that I don't deserve such blessings. I suppose no one deserves all the blessings he or she has in life, but I have so many more blessings than other people that it makes me wonder why. I've never asked, "Why me?" about getting my illness. Instead, I often ask, "Why me?" in regard to all these blessings in my life. I have no idea if there is some overall fairness to any of it, but the point is that I feel incredibly fortunate.

I continue. "The biggest blessing, and this also comes from my faith, is that I was an atheist before I was ill. Without my illness, I may never have become a Christian. All things being equal, I would rather not have my illness. However, all things are not equal, and I would never have become Christian had I not become ill. I don't think God wanted me to become ill, but I consider it the biggest blessing of my life. I would rather choose my life now, to be ill and Christian, than to be normal and an atheist. Every day I thank God for my life. That is not to say I don't have tough times and get hopeless; I do. But, when I sit down and think about it, I would rather have this illness. Honestly, I have never heard anyone with my condition say that before. Maybe that is why I'm so happy, because I don't dread it and I'm not thinking, 'Woe is me.' With faith, I keep up hope. I believe that with God in my life, all things are possible. That doesn't mean I get everything I want, but it allows me to beat the statistics. Even though there is a doom-and-gloom prognosis with schizophrenia, I beat the statistics every day. I have no more willpower than anyone else with the illness, but with God in my life, I keep beating the statistics and that gives me hope. It keeps me happy. My life is pretty good; I don't know anyone who has a better life than I do."

"*Except me,*" Benji says.

"Even you. I think I have a better life than you do. And you probably think you have a better life than I do too."

He begins to laugh.

"I believe," I say, "that I have the best life of anybody who is or has lived in the entire world. I'm pretty thrilled about that."

Benji, while still laughing, says, "*I think you are overly thrilled right now.*"

"I'm overly thrilled, probably."

"*I would like to expand upon something you already mentioned. You said that you have this perspective now. But you didn't have it the day you were diagnosed, did you?*"

"No, not even close."

"*It wasn't like, 'Life's great: schizophrenia!'*"

"No, no," I say, "not at all."

"*You talked about how religion came into your life slowly. Other than that, how did you turn from 'Life is awful' to 'Life is pretty good and I'm blessed?'*"

"Two things come to mind. One was that in the period after being diagnosed I would listen to talk radio at home in my room. There is a radio host named Dennis Prager. He does a three-hour-long program in the mornings and speaks a lot on morality and things like that. Well, on Fridays he does a show, in the middle hour, called 'The Happiness Hour.' He has done it every Friday for many, many years. He would talk about how to find happiness, and a lot of that resonated with me, like being thankful for things. From his show, I gained a better perspective on life. That, along with listening to some of his other hours, helped me believe in God. I gained more from his radio show than from therapy for those few weeks. The other thing that gave me my current perspective was something a guy said to me one night when I was out drinking. We were talking about how lucky we were in life. And he said, 'We are not lucky; we are blessed.' That line resonated with me, because I realized that it wasn't just good fortune and being lucky, but God helping us out when we needed it. That realization struck a chord with me. I think about it all the time."

"For someone who has just learned the diagnosis or fears he or she will come down with the diagnosis of schizophrenia, what kind of advice would you have to develop coping mechanisms?"

"I'm thinking of an advertisement, 'Got God?'—sort of like the 'Got Milk?' advertisements. I think they need some kind of faith in their life to keep up hope; without it all you have is the doom and gloom. I think that is why people with schizophrenia become hyperreligious—what else do they have? It is that bad. However, you also need help from outside. My other advice would be to get diagnosed early and take your meds, because that means a better outcome. You always have to take your meds. If you don't, you're going to get sick. Who cares if you get fat? Take your meds. Who cares if you get restless legs? Take your meds."

CHAPTER 21:
SOME THOUGHTS V

A s I am getting healthier, I am finding the most confusing thing about my illness is the role of faith in my life. My coming to faith has allowed me to embrace my illness and cope, but at the same time, because I didn't have faith before my illness, I can never tell what is real faith and what is crazy faith. It goes back to the old question of what is religion and what is delusion. It is similar to Benji's experience of not knowing the difference between grandiosity and normal dreams.

Some people would respond to this problem that I'm having with my faith by throwing out all their spiritual thoughts as crazy. That is a mistake. Most of my paranoid ideas involved government spies, and just because they were crazy thoughts, that doesn't mean government spies don't exist. So I am just trying to keep level headed about my spirituality.

I frequently talk to a pastor at my church when I'm trying to discern what is real in terms of spiritual beliefs. He is genuinely interested in my plight and tries to help as much as he can, but in all honesty, he is about as clueless as I am. At the moment, there doesn't seem to be a way to separate religion from madness as far as my personal faith experiences go. But I do take comfort in knowing that there are normal people of faith, so the idea of having a spiritual relationship with God isn't a nonstarter.

If the church had a better understanding of mental illness, it could lead the way in securing better lives for people with mental illness. The church has been slumbering on this issue, but in recent years there has been some traction. I know of about five different local churches with programs specifically for the mentally ill. That is an encouraging step in the right direction.

Even on days when my passion for my faith is waning, I still find myself dreaming of becoming a professional evangelist. I don't think I have the gifts for it, and I know that I don't have the education, but I feel strongly about the positive impact my spirituality has had on my life. I actually love my life. That is amazing to be able to say. Just a few years ago I wanted nothing but to die. I thought of suicide day and night. But today, I feel like rejoicing. Perhaps that could be my evangelical message. I wouldn't talk to people about heavy theology; instead, I would show them how God has transformed my life. In the very least, that could be a start.

CHAPTER 22:
FUTURE OUTLOOK

I watched the movie *Proof* last night. Despite having some well-known actors—Gwyneth Paltrow and Anthony Hopkins—it seems like an independent flick. I had seen it before, but I think it has become my new favorite movie. The story is about a woman in her mid-20s who fears that she is about to develop schizophrenia like her father did. The acting is great, but the writing is even better. As I was watching the movie, I kept seeing in the character all these telltale signs of the prodrome, the lead-up to developing the first psychotic episode of schizophrenia. In many ways, my demeanor and behavior were similar to the character in the movie.

The movie indirectly poses a fascinating question: Can someone with severe mental illness accomplish something extraordinary? I think I know the answer (yes), but I know it in my heart and not in my head. This belief is what sustains me. It is the knowledge held in my heart that something extraordinary is possible from me. Without that knowledge, without that hope, I would be a statistic.

I would be yet another data point promoting the dismal prognosis of this illness.

I never thought I'd really drive again, certainly not comfortably, but I just drove myself to Starbucks. Benji met me here, and we got our drinks and sat down in the back on a couch and the armchair next to it. I take out my recorder, and we begin.

"Today," I say, "is Monday. We are back at Starbucks at 50th and France, having teas today, changing it up a bit. I thought we would talk today about the future, about our futures, and what we will tackle next. Benji, what are the next steps in your life right now?"

"*Well,*" he says, "*these conversations have allowed me to step back from my illness. Looking at what I have experienced has helped me see a clearer picture of who I am today. I have a better sense of what is realistically obtainable. These conversations have been like a launching pad for what I can accomplish from here on out. They have forced me to look in, and now I'm ready to look out again. I feel that I'm not limited as much as the literature says I should be or how my peers thought I might be. I am not as limited as I thought I might be. At first, I had a negative outlook concerning my illness. I once again have lofty ambitions, but this time I think I'm following them for the right reasons. I am still enrolled at a technical college, studying plants and landscape design. If I finish that program, I hope to get into a landscape architecture graduate program that will build off my degree. I would like to one day be a landscape architect and be renowned for making beautiful landscapes and gardens, because that is where my passion is. Five years from now I'm not*" sure if I will be that far along in accomplishing my goal; however, maybe 10 years from now, I will. I can see myself doing something like that."

He takes a drink of his tea. "*Before this I was very impatient. I wanted all my gratifications as soon as I thought of them. Through all my mania I was consumed with conspicuous consumption. The idea of getting things and gratifying myself immediately was my only instinct. I remember one day I was in the process of maxing out my credit card and bought a $2,000 TV. When I went to the ATM after this purchase, I couldn't take money out with my debit card—not because there was no money, but because I couldn't focus enough to remember my PIN number. I kept keying in numbers until the machine ate my card. To curb my impulsive spending, I have come up with this new system where, if I can't buy something with the cash in my pocket, then maybe I should think twice about buying it. This plan is one way I have changed the way I do things. I don't use a credit card anymore. I either write a check or use cash I withdraw on a weekly basis as part of the allowance I give myself. Most of the time, this approach works out great. However, a couple weeks ago I was going to buy something that cost about $1,000, and once again I put in the wrong bank code at the ATM. I knew immediately that I shouldn't buy it. I bought it anyway.*"

"Did you have any friends telling you not to buy it?" I ask with a smile.

"*Yeah, you told me not to buy it.*" Benji begins to chuckle. "*I once again wanted an electronic item: a computer. I returned it the next day and had to pay a restocking charge that was like $80, but still paying the restocking charge was better than spending the $800. Obviously,*"

I still battle with my illness every day. That incident occurred only six weeks ago. I realize that my bipolar disorder will never go away. It doesn't go away, and that realization is something I live with every day. I have to make up little games so I can live with it in a way that allows me to constantly be in tune and check what is wrong. I am always making impromptu decisions that can save me a lot of money, save my health, or save the emotions of others."

"With bipolar, the suicide rate is about 20 percent, and many more attempt it. Being here with me now, do you consider yourself a survivor?"

"I've never contemplated suicide," he says, *"and I hope I never will. The threat of so deep a depression is one of the biggest reasons I have never gone off the medicine. I've experienced lows, but I have read and heard of others having deep depressions that last half a year or even years at a time. These types of depression are the kinds that the famous painters would get. As a result, they wouldn't paint anything for like three years. I haven't experienced anything like that, and I never want to, which is all the more motivation to stay on the regimen of medicine. I'm doing everything to keep me from taking my own life, because suicide hurts so many people close to you. Maybe it has crossed my mind, but it was nothing I contemplated or thought through. I am saddened to hear those kinds of statistics. In many respects, I consider myself a survivor because I'm beating the statistics and avoiding what people say I should be experiencing with bipolar."*

"Benji," I say, "you said that you are no longer into immediate consumption, and that you can be more patient. It seems to be something that has changed in you as you learned to deal with the illness. Well, my illness has changed my outlook on life too."

I take a drink of my tea. "One thing I realized was that I didn't know anything about mental illness before I was sick, and it opened my eyes to the plight of people who are going through tough times. Here in Minnesota, 47 percent of the homeless have mental illness. Before my illness, I would have thought that the homeless were on the street because they were too lazy to work. Now I think, 'These people are sick and need help.' I'm more compassionate toward them, and it is a changed outlook to realize that people have some serious problems. As a child I was guarded from seeing that people had serious problems. The few problems I did see were relationship problems and such but not serious, life-changing ones. That is one way my illness has had a positive impact: I'm a different and better person now."

"*That's great,*" Benji says. "*Have you tried to raise awareness about mental illness?*"

"Yes, I have been doing a lot of things to raise awareness. There's my volunteer work with the Barbara Schneider Foundation and with the police officer training. I also speak to community groups, church groups, and NAMI groups. A year ago I even tried to start a nonprofit organization of my own that would educate college students on mental illness, because the earlier you treat mental illness the better the outcome. That endeavor eventually collapsed; I wasn't healthy enough to go through with it. However, I still do the support groups at my church. As for the next steps in my life, I'm starting my publishing company. So far, it is just at the dreaming stage right now, because it will be so hard for me to get it going. I mean, I can hardly take showers in the morning, so getting motivated to do anything is an everyday struggle. Nevertheless, I'm excited about it, and I'm going to try for it. If it fails, it fails. I asked you if you felt like a survivor. I consider myself a survivor, too. I'm going to make it. I feel happy about that. I've been through hell, but I intend to keep going. I think that battling my illness is heroic. To me, you are a hero, too. These are some of the toughest illnesses that there are."

I take a drink of my tea and then turn off the recorder. Ever since I watched *Proof,* I have been thinking about numbers. I know that I will never be able to do anything serious in math now, but I can still understand the ideas of mathematics. All day, I have been thinking about statistics.

It seems that everyone is concerned about statistics, or more exactly, concerned about how others use statistics. People influence, bias, and even lie with them. When I was younger, whenever I was in a heated debate and someone tried to use statistics to support a point, I would always say, "Oh yeah, well, 75 percent of all statistics are made up." That rebuttal usually silenced my adversary, or at least caused a chuckle and lightened the mood. I used to care about people lying with statistics, but what concerns me now is the truths people tell with them.

The truth sometimes hurts, and, when you are talking about the prognosis of schizophrenia, statistics can be frightening. The prognosis is gloomy. But I know something now, something I could never have known while I was in the depths of despair. Had someone told me, I wouldn't have believed him or her. It is that if you have hope, statistics become irrelevant. With hope, the numbers nailing down your likely course have been pried up, freeing your future to be guided by your desires and not that of any illness.

I used to worry that I wouldn't be able to accomplish anything great in this life. How could I? I have schizophrenia, after all. However, these worries are past now. They have withered away, along with my suicidal thoughts. What occupies my mind today is one question: "What else?" In short, what else can I accomplish? What else can I do that is even greater? This peppers even my most incoherent, graphomanic journal entries. The unknown yet promising potential for greater accomplishments is sweet indeed. I embrace the freedom that comes from being liberated from statistics. I don't know what my future holds, but I feel as if I am standing on some great mountain looking out over the world: I see all the wonderful possibilities of my unknown future. I'm facing my future with eyes wide open, and in complete wonderment and gratitude, I can do nothing but ask, "What else?"

Where We Are Now

Since our last conversation, Benji got a summer landscaping job. He and his barista girlfriend split up after dating for several months. In the fall, instead of returning to technical school, Benji landed a job in California in the horticultural field. He is now living there and has met a woman. Our conversations continue over the phone, but they aren't quite the same. I do feel a significant void in my life with my best friend gone. Benji's absence, however, means that he is pursuing his dreams. Right now he is happy and healthy, and so I know another one of my prayers has been answered.

As for me, I have been doing a lot—giving speeches, promoting my book, changing the world (well, two out of three isn't bad). I have also created a blog that can be viewed as the afterword to this book. My Regular & Decaf blog is on my Web site, www.regularanddecaf.com. You will also find photos and other relevant info on the site. When you stop by, drop me a line.